The Disruptive Pupil in the Secondary School

Editors CLIVE JONES-DAVIES
Assistant Education Officer (Special Education)
Cleveland
and
RONALD G. CAVE
Senior Education Officer (Inspection and
Advisory Services)
Cambridgeshire

WARD LOCK EDUCATIONAL

ISBN 0 7062 3457 X paperback
0 7062 3456 1 hardback

First published 1976

Set in 10 on 11 point Baskerville
and printed by Willmer Brothers Limited, Birkenhead
for Ward Lock Educational
116 Baker Street, London W1M 2BB
Made in Great Britain

Contents

The views expressed by the editors and contributors are personal and not necessarily those of their employing authorities and institutions.

Introduction

RONALD G. CAVE

During the first year following the raising of the school leaving age it was almost impossible to open an educational periodical without reading alarming reports of increasing disruption in schools. Making a random selection from copies of the *Times Educational Supplement*, which lie on my desk as I write this introduction, I find that a survey and digest of Inner London Education Authority district inspectors' reports says that truancy and bad behaviour in the first year after the raising of the school leaving age in Inner London were not due to boredom but to factors beyond the schools' control. The report blames the present problems of pupil behaviour on the shortage and high turnover of teachers, part-time schooling, teacher resentment over pay, the lack of staff for craft and vocational subjects, the shortage of educational welfare officers, social workers and careers teachers, the numbers of young and inexperienced teachers and lack of housing. The Berkshire Association of Secondary Heads reports an increasing number of disruptive children in the county's schools and blames the deterioration on the problems in society in general, confused standards in the home and lack of resources in social and welfare services. They conclude that 'there is a serious danger this degree of disruption will escalate because evidence suggests it is not being dealt with effectively and that staff, pupils and parents are in danger of becoming demoralized.' It would be all too easy but certainly tedious to cite numerous other reports from Local Education Authorities and professional associations, but perhaps one more example will underline the fact that there appears to be a fair degree of consensus about the causes of, if not the answers to, the problem of disruptive pupils. In the same week as the Berkshire evidence appeared in the press the Essex Association of the National Union of Teachers called for a new custodial order which would enable local authorities to deal with 'the small minority of excessively disruptive pupils who seriously impair the educational progress of the majority.' The Essex teachers believe that high staff turnover, the shortage of teachers, a high proportion of inexperienced teachers, staff absenteeism in secondary schools, difficulties of adjusting to new teaching methods and pupil-teacher relationships, unsuitable curricula and the shortage of materials are all thought to be possible factors of disruption. The report

5

urges, however, that the whole question of disruption be kept in proportion, and one of the prime objectives of this present book is to attempt to do exactly that.

Obviously the authors of the following chapters are dealing with an aspect of school life which is seriously complicated by the difficulty of exact definition. In his introductory chapters, the co-editor draws attention to the need to distinguish between disturbing as opposed to disturbed children, and other contributions stress that there is no necessary connection between disruption and deprivation. Even within the same staffroom there may well be contrasting views as to what constitutes disruptive behaviour. Brian Davies emphasizes this in his own inimitable manner when he writes that one man's disruption may approximate to another's peak teaching experience. As a sociologist he also reminds us that deviance inheres not essentially in either the qualities of the act or the actor but in the process of definition by legitimately empowered others.

No foolish claim is made that this collection of papers will provide easy answers to the problems caused by disruptive secondary-school students. However, a variety of possible approaches is discussed by people working in the field which at the least may make a modest contribution to partial solutions. In general the views expressed are optimistic and yet practical and firmly grounded in common sense. The inescapable fact that neither educational problems appear to be so well defined, nor the answers so apparently obvious, as they once seemed to be is no excuse for inhibition on the part of responsible educationists. That we cannot provide immediate answers to the problem of disruption at this stage is no reason to assume that progress cannot be made in common-sense terms towards workable solutions. On the other hand it would be irresponsible not to recognize the very real difficulties and to underestimate the fact that this is one of those areas of educational debate where it is often the best who exhibit an understandable uncertainty and the worst who are filled with a passionate conviction. There must be some optimum answers to the problem of disruptive young people in a democratic society, and if the teaching profession doesn't find them, who will?

Ronald G. Cave
Cambridge, May 1975

1 An overview and definition of the problem

CLIVE JONES-DAVIES

That there has been a significant deterioration in the behaviour of children in secondary schools appears to be beyond dispute. The press, television and radio often report disruption not just of local but of national consequence. Nor does the educational press fail to contribute and its correspondence columns especially reflect the great concern shown by educationists about this particular problem. Psychiatrists dealing with adolescence, educational psychologists, school medical officers and teachers seem generally agreed that disturbed behaviour by children has become much more widespread. In addition to the increase in the frequency of problem behaviour in schools, it may also be noted that the more extreme forms of maladjusted behaviour have increased in intensity. Psychiatrists report an increased number of suicide attempts and cases of self-mutilation by children. This problem extends beyond the secondary school to primary schools, and even teachers in infant schools express concern at the prevalence of antisocial behaviour amongst children in their schools. A recent study by a school medical officer of the opinions of head teachers about the integration of handicapped pupils in ordinary schools showed that the greatest problem was thought to be that posed by children with adjustment difficulties. These, it was reported, are now both more widespread and more intensive and despite the reduction in the size of classes the difficulty is considerably greater than hitherto (Jones-Davies 1974).

However, it should be noted that the surveys already made of disruption in schools show that only a small minority of pupils actually resort to serious violence and disruption. L. F. Lowenstein (1975) in his study reports a figure of 0.64 incidents of violence per 100 pupils in secondary schools and a figure of 4.48 incidents of disruptions per 100 pupils in such schools. A survey of violence, indiscipline and vandalism carried out by the Association of Education Committees in 1973 on behalf of the Department of Education and Science recorded 7.68 incidents of violence per 10,000 pupils in secondary schools and 3.81 incidents of 'rowdyism' per 10,000 pupils (DES 1975). Nevertheless, the effect of even a small minority on the working of a school can be highly disruptive and it is true that such incidents have a cumulative influence which over a period of time can disturb a large number of pupils who themselves might not resort to serious violence or disruption but whose behaviour can become unsettled.

Disruption of the normal routine of schools is caused by a wide range of differing behaviours which varies from spasmodic interruption of class work to incidents of extreme physical violence offered to both staff and fellow-pupils. Teachers report that even petty interruptions of class teaching have increased so that behaviour which was usually confined to one or two pupils is now characteristic of many children who disrupt a particular lesson by clowning or by failing to have essential equipment. Such incidents are in themselves trivial but their cumulative effect is to disturb the progress of lessons. It is now considerably more difficult to eliminate such behaviour since children are less responsive to the directions of teachers and more inclined to defiance. Petty incidents frequently act as the spark for a major confrontation. The more publicized incidents of disruption, of course, are those which involve violent behaviour, especially when this includes the use of offensive weapons, the prevalence of which has also increased significantly. Whereas, in the past, few teachers were actually physically attacked by pupils, such behaviour is now frequently reported.

Violent attacks on other pupils, of a far worse nature than the schoolyard brawls of yesteryear, which in almost every case harmed neither of the protagonists, have also increased, although less sharply. Physical violence is often accompanied by violence of the tongue, which is itself much more prevalent than hitherto. Teachers are frequently subjected to abuse and threats which are usually obscene, because this is the easiest form of such invective.

Vandalism is much more in evidence in schools today than in the past, and extensive damage to the fabric of buildings and to fittings, especially in lavatories and other places where supervision is less easy than in the corridors and classrooms, may be observed. The defacing of walls with graffiti, especially with aggressive slogans such as 'Man. United rule O.K.', is now commonplace. To blame this form of vandalism on the advent of spray canisters and felt pens is unrealistic: it is the expressive urge that has increased, not the opportunity for such expression.

Truancy is also considered by many as a form of disruption, especially when measures to counter it are ineffective and pupils see how easy it is. Truancy brings the school's authority into disrepute, and in addition the unofficial comings and goings of children, at times other than those of a normal school day, foster indiscipline and interrupt normal routine. Children have always truanted and the causes of truancy have ranged from the very real personal problems of some children to the 'occasional holiday' indulged in by others as a relief from the, to them, lack of adventure of the school day. For a number of pupils, however, truancy now represents a flouting of the school's authority and a denial of the utility of school for their purposes. We do not intend in this book to deal with truancy in detail since we are concerned with disruptive behaviour within the school, but it must be remembered that the absence of some children contributes to the indiscipline and uncooperativeness of other children who remain at school.

The examples of disruptive behaviour quoted above are themselves an appropriate area for research, since it is almost certainly the case that children do not choose certain types of behaviour at random but develop a 'style' of disruption appropriate to their particular problems. Discussions with teachers and others concerned with disruptive behaviour have tended to reinforce the view that such behaviour is a personal activity; little evidence exists, in my experience, of collective, organized, systematic disruption. Reference has been made in speeches and in the press to the possibility of a concerted attempt by anarchist organizations to enroll young people at school and motivate them to disrupt schools as symbols of the society which is their wider target. In the absence of more specific evidence than is available at present, it is reasonable to assume that the vandalism and violence that are becoming more prevalent in schools are personal protests, legitimate or otherwise. The only evidence of systematic disruption at present is the case of individual children who may deliberately set out on a course of bad behaviour, hoping to be suspended from school and anticipating a consequent relaxation of the regulations governing compulsory school attendance. Some young people have admitted that they have sought suspension from school with the misinformed opinion that the Local Education Authority would agree to their entering employment. Most disruptive behaviour, however, is intermittent and spontaneous, though this is not to say that it is unaffected by what is happening in society in general.

Causes of disruptive behaviour
Indiscipline in school has been attributed to a large number of causes. A recent publication by one of the major teachers' unions lists twenty-six separate but not always unconnected reasons for the decline of discipline in schools (NAS 1974). There have always been disruptive children, and some of the reasons now suggested for indiscipline have also existed for some considerable time. Social and economic deprivation has always affected a proportion of the school population and has resulted in some cases in extremes of anti-social behaviour. It is these children also who, in the main, have suffered from having educationally unsupportive parents.

The disruption which causes concern today, however, is by no means confined to children from deprived backgrounds. Furthermore, factors such as inadequate school buildings, unfavourable pupil-teacher ratios and inappropriate or unavailable equipment have always existed. Indeed, it might well be argued that present-day schools are significantly more favoured in these respects than schools of a few years ago. Similarly, although still open to some criticism, the training of teachers has improved and is unlikely to produce a greater proportion of poor teachers than in previous generations. At worst, such factors only contribute to the problem or in some cases are the initial spark which leads the child to resort to unconforming behaviour. It is unlikely that either singly or accumulatively they have caused the significant acceleration in the incidence of disruptive behaviour and the increasing inability of some schools to manage such problems.

Despite the optimism of some individuals, it appears that schools are affected by society rather than themselves influencing society directly. Sociologists have described how schools are microcosmic representations of the societies which support them and that the values and mores of schools are, in the main, those of the wider society. It is in what is happening in society today that we may find the real reasons for the changes that have resulted in indiscipline and disruption in schools. During the last ten years society has become spectacularly more disharmonious. It is undeniable that, with the exception of periods of actual war, there is considerably more violence in evidence today than ever before. National and religious confrontations either smoulder at the level of guerilla warfare or burst into the flames of real war before an uneasy peace is achieved. Also well publicized are countless examples of individual atrocities, often resulting in considerable loss of life and damage to property, carried out in the name of causes which in the past resorted to less violent and even legal means of furthering their ends. Such causes have always had some violent supporters. Today, however, far more of their adherents resort to extreme forms of violence using the sophisticated equipment now available. The failure of governments, either singly or collectively, to prevent such disruption points to the brittleness of authority and suggests the ineffectuality of laws and codes of inter-personal behaviour. Though governments often assert their authority and do all in their power to curb such violence they are properly limited by codes of conduct which pertain even in war but which leave the advantage with determined and unscrupulous individuals.

The questioning of authority is an acceptable and essential element of progress. Today, however, protest appears to be a style of life which depends not on constitutional and legitimate processes but on violence and on the destruction of the values or system under attack by a policy of disruption.

Without doubt, the behaviour of children is affected by such events. The increased permissiveness of society, especially in sexual morality and the portrayal of violence in literature and films on television, has been suggested as a further cause of disruptive behaviour in schools. The precise effect of the 'new morality' on the behaviour of schoolchildren cannot yet be accurately assessed, but it is likely that the conflict between what was and what is now seen as acceptable behaviour will have repercussions on the conduct of young people at school. Even more important, however, is the element of questioning that is involved in permissiveness whereby previously held standards are called into doubt and alternative standards offered in their place. This questioning is akin to the more violent challenging of governmental authority already described in that it too seeks to bring about a new order. The fact that previously undisputed and unchallenged institutions and standards are now being attacked probably has a very real effect upon the behaviour of young people at school who find themselves at loggerheads with those in authority over them. Furthermore the glamourization of such challenges by the media affects the natural aggressiveness of young people and causes it to degenerate into excessive violence.

Schools are by no means the only areas in which this conflict may be observed. So-called 'soccer hooliganism' is also in part the product of challenge to authority. The behaviour of soccer players *vis-à-vis* the authority of the referee is reflected in the behaviour of young football fans towards the police and to other symbols of authority such as property.

It is interesting to note that in the many accounts of disruptive behaviour in school very few references are made to the theft of personal property from other children. Although from time to time serious incidents of aggressiveness against individual children are reported, these tend to be less frequent than attacks upon teachers. Thus the target of present violence and vandalism appears to be people and property associated with authority. Systematic research is of course needed to support this theory, though crime figures for England and Wales do offer some evidence. In the first six months of 1974, there was an overall increase of 20 per cent in reported crime compared with the same period in 1973. Whereas the incidence of criminal damage rose by 28 per cent and of offences of theft and handling stolen goods and of burglary by 23 and 22 per cent respectively, the incidence of violence rose by only 3 per cent and that of sexual offences dropped by 6 per cent. In the corresponding period in 1973, offences of violence rose by 21.6 per cent over 1972. Thus offences against property, seen as a symbol of the established system, increased whilst offences against the private individual decreased.

The change in the political and economic status of the adolescent has also doubtless had an effect on behaviour in secondary school. An adolescent's standing out of school is considerably higher than in school. Whereas out of school the adolescent has risen to near parity with adults in terms of economic freedom and certainly to parity as the target of advertising, inside school he remains in a secondary position in relation to adults. Improved leisure facilities and high-quality possessions, such as stereophonic equipment and clothing, put him in a favoured position in comparison with adults, who may have somewhat greater financial freedom but have in addition greater financial responsibilities.

The normal school situation depends heavily upon the submissiveness of one partner in the learning activity to the authority of the other. The submissive partner may well question the authority of the dominant partner and will naturally seek greater freedom within the learning situation. In later chapters we will discuss the nature of adolescence and its essential striving towards independence and a well-established personal identity; at this point it is sufficient to say that, whereas the normal learning activity is a process which enlarges both partners and in the long run diminishes neither, some individuals, influenced by what is happening in society at large, may now be becoming intolerant of it. Some schools have already attempted to reorganize their structure of authority so that this confrontation may be seen to be unnecessary. Such changes, however, should be the product of very careful consideration and examination of the elements involved in the situation. The sudden substitution of a *laissez-faire* non-authoritarian régime for the more traditional organization involving a hierarchical structure of responsibilities might well be the cause of indiscipline in the initial period. Greater consultation with staff and even with pupils will quite properly be the pattern of the future, but the demands of some teachers, primarily those who led protests in their colleges of education and universities, for a greater share of responsibility for administration and for the diminution of the authority of the head and senior staff can only contribute to disruption.

Finally, and this is by no means less important than the considerations discussed above, it must be admitted that disruption in secondary schools often results from the failure of schools to provide a relevant curriculum for many of their children. Certainly in the case of the less able children, and also in the case of able children who are none the less reluctant to learn, the post-primary curriculum is to a very large extent irrelevant. Such children fail to realize the utility of even its most relevant aspects and consequently become antipathetic and often disruptive. This was not a new problem, but the raising of the school leaving age accentuated it; that very many schools failed to do anything more than just contain the fifteen to sixteen-year-olds for whom they were responsible made it even worse. This subject will be discussed later in this introductory section and also in other contributions to this book.

The problems of disruptive behaviour faced by secondary schools are the result of many interacting and complex factors. This chapter, by summarizing these factors, is intended as an introduction to later chapters, which discuss methods of preventing and managing disruptive behaviour.

Disturbed or disturbing children

Any discussion of the problem of disruptive children in secondary schools must decide whether such children may legitimately be categorized as 'maladjusted' and therefore receive special educational treatment as such. I believe that disruptive children present problems which at least in part are similar to those presented by maladjusted children but that such children are not pathologically disturbed in the same sense as maladjusted children. Estimates of the incidence of maladjustment and the conflicting definitions of the term make any decision to include or exclude from the 'maladjusted' category of disruptive children merely a matter of opinion. It appears, however, that on the whole the pattern of behaviour of disruptive (disturbing) children does not fit the criteria of severe personality disturbance and emotional damage which characterize truly maladjusted (disturbed) children. It is necessary to differentiate between those children who suffer long-term adjustment difficulties and those whose problems of unsettledness are transient. There may well be amongst disruptive children a number who are in fact pathologically disturbed, but these are a minority. It may be said of these children as a whole that their difficulties are not such that they would automatically be referred to a school psychological service or to a child guidance service.

At this time it is impossible to estimate accurately the extent of the disruption caused in secondary schools by disturbing as opposed to disturbed children – such an estimate would have to be made on the basis of a national survey. The various estimates of the problem of maladjustment made in recent surveys such as that by the National Children's Bureau and in the Isle of Wight study have little relevance; the conventional adjustment questionnaires used in such surveys need at the very least to be supplemented by some other technique to establish the motivation which underlies disruptive behaviour. It should not, however, be forgotten that the ordinary school as well as the special maladjusted school plays a considerable role in the management and education of ascertained maladjusted children: the official *Statistics of Education Volume 1: Schools 1974* states that 3,566 children ascertained as maladjusted were attending ordinary schools, only 1,276 of these being special units (DES 1975). The problem becomes even greater if one accepts the following operational definition of maladjustment (Michael Brittain 1970):

> Those children are maladjusted whose behaviour is developing in ways which have a bad effect on themselves or their fellows, and cannot be remedied without specialist psychiatric or psychological help, by their parents, teachers or other adults in ordinary contact with them.

From this definition and the statistics provided in *The Health of the School Child 1971 to 1972* (DES 1974), which states that 74,700 children received treatment under child guidance arrangements during that year but that only 16,130 (2,133 of them in units in ordinary schools) were receiving special educational treatment or awaiting places at maladjusted schools, it is evident that nearly four out of every five 'maladjusted' children were receiving education in ordinary classes in ordinary schools. The significance of these figures for schools in their efforts to cope with the problem of disruptive children is obvious and the schools' present difficulties with such children should be seen in the context of these statistics.

The children with whom this book is concerned, however, are not those whom one would normally wish to place either in special schools or in special day units for maladjusted children.

If one accepts the recommendation of the working party on children with special needs, reported in *Living with Handicap*, the distinction between disturbing and disturbed children becomes easier. The working party recognized the need to revise the term maladjustment and suggested that the term 'emotional handicap' should be substituted (Younghusband *et al* 1970). The great majority of disturbing children are not in fact emotionally disturbed in the sense that they require special educational treatment, although it could well be argued that they are maladjusted in that they are out of step with the environment of their school.

Adolescence and disruption

Many writers, though none better than E. H. Ericson, have stressed that it is the function of adolescence to achieve independence and thereby a separate and personal individual identity (Ericson 1965). This involves rejecting the submissive role of the pre-adolescent, who depends on the dominant and authoritarian agencies of home and school, and the establishment of a separate, self-directing identity with emotional, social and physical autonomy. Insecure parents and unsure schools, guarded in their attitudes and threatened by this change in the young person with whom they are dealing, overreact and reassert their tendency to inflexibility and refusal to change, itself a psychologically interesting phenomenon. This contributes to the conflicts in schools and homes. In terms of adolescent psychology, disruption may be described as a confrontation and a power struggle between the emerging personality of the adolescent and the school's desire to retain authority within the learning situation. Very many schools, and parents too, guide and provide opportunities for adolescents to achieve a satisfying and functionally successful sense of self. Inevitably, however, since adolescence is essentially a state of disequilibrium, communication between the young person and the school and/or the home does not always allow for a considered and understanding shift of standpoint on the part of the latter. All too frequently schools and parents find themselves in a situation in which they have to assert their authority, although they are aware that in so doing they may be exacerbating the crisis that exists between them and the adolescent. Unfortunately such conflicts create a stressful period for the adolescent which prevents him from establishing that identity for himself which would make him a more effective partner. These stressful situations result in what Ericson has called 'role diffusion', whereby no firm sense of self is established by the individual and his allegiances are dissipated, resulting in half-held beliefs and conflicting attitudes which make him, in more adult eyes, an 'irrational' individual (Ericson 1968).

Adolescence is an aggressive period, which is not to say that its nature is either violent or destructive. The aggression of adolescence is its assertiveness. Aggressiveness in terms of violence has been regarded by some, including Lorenz (1966), as an inherent part of human nature and others, such as Arendt (1970), have stressed that all men have violent tendencies since these are essential in the achievement of certain ends. In their book *Violence, Monkeys and Man* (1968), on the other hand C. Russell and W. M. S. Russell stress that 'man is not, as some contend, innately aggressive irrespective of environmental influences' and that violent behaviour by human beings and also by animals, is the natural response to intolerable frustrations (Russell and Russell 1968). It is unnecessary to decide here on the relative merits of these conflicting views, since both appear to be true of the assertiveness of adolescence. In the adolescent's attempt to establish his own worth and a secure ego, his assertiveness sometimes degenerates into violence against people or things. It should be remembered that his motivation for independence and autonomy is strong and that his ability to deal with frustration is weak. Authority is therefore by definition the adolescent's opponent, whether it be the authority of his parents, his teachers or of society, the police for instance. The adolescent is not in continuous conflict with authority, nor is he its enemy, since frequently the school, the home and society at large provide him with the right experiences properly to develop his sense of self. All too often, however, he is cast as a rebel and further alienated by his elders' rigid attitudes: I heard a psychiatrist dealing with adolescents remark recently that the more he had become involved with their problems the more he himself became alienated from society.

Disruption and an anti-school and anti-authority attitude
I believe therefore that disruption is the adolescent's response in the confrontation between himself and the authority of the school. This response is of course complicated and reinforced by the disruption that exists in society and the loosening of the bonds of authority. This is by no means a simplistic view of the problem since the individual nature of each adolescent's needs means that each incident or series of incidents of disruption is an arena of conflicting attitudes, motives and emotions. Furthermore, each act of disruption may be either a piece of goal-directed behaviour in which the individual seeks a particular end of self-aggrandizement or a defensive manoeuvre against an attempt, in his eyes, to reduce his status. Combinations of these may also be observed in certain acts of disruption in which the individual is acting from a sense of frustration because of a limitation imposed on his ego-development and seeks to overcome this frustration by some satisfaction achieved through assertive behaviour. Such attitudes have been defined by Katz and Stotland (1959) as 'ego defensive attitudes', when the individual attempts to safeguard his sense of self, and 'ego instrumental attitudes', when the individual attempts to extend that concept of self. The majority of adolescents will develop a concept of self without resorting to extremes of conflict, but, conversely, those who are in any sense threatened will develop this attitude in terms of extreme ideas and emotions which find expression in acts of violence against people and property.

Schools have always managed to contain children who have been antipathetic to school, and the adoption of an anti-school attitude or a cluster of such attitudes by children at school has not in the past brought about the extremes of behaviour with which they have to deal today. In a study of the attitude to school of two groups of boys in a secondary modern school, I showed that whereas the academic success of the group more favourably inclined to school was greater than that of the antipathetic group, this latter group nevertheless had certain characteristics which made them valuable members of the school community (Jones-Davies 1965).

A study which I undertook later of a group of delinquent boys in a remand home and classifying centre who demonstrated a negative social evaluation system in terms of a cluster of negative social attitudes showed, however, that certain adolescents, characterized by personality traits such as egocentricity, can in fact become so antagonistic towards society that they are unable to discriminate between key figures in society and therefore evaluate everything negatively (Jones-Davies 1968). This type of attitude is that held by the extreme of the disruptive children at present in secondary schools. Numerically such children are few, but their effect in any class is most profound, both because of the disruption they themselves cause and because of their influence on other children. Although not all disruptive children develop the gelled antagonistic attitudes of such delinquents, if the stresses of adolescence have been sufficiently severe their antagonisms to certain elements of society, which may include the school or certain parts of it, may become deeply entrenched.

This discussion of adolescence and disruption, brief though it has had to be, has, it is hoped, established that disruption should be seen not in terms of an emotional maladjustment, (indeed the emotional component of disruption may well be at an appropriate level to the frustration felt by the adolescent) but as an essential characteristic of the inevitable confrontation between schools and their adolescent pupils. Disruption may be instigated by ambition or frustration or by both.

References

ARENDT, H. (1970) *On Violence* London: Allen Lane

BRITTAIN, M. (1970) *The Epidemiology of Maladjustment* London: Royal Society of Health

DES (1974) *The Health of the School Child 1971 to 1972* HMSO

DES (1975) *Statistics of Education Volume 1: Schools* London: HMSO

ERICSON, E. H. (1965) *Childhood and Society* Harmondsworth: Penguin

ERICSON, E. H. (1968) *Identity: Youth and Crisis* London: Faber

JONES-DAVIES, D. C. (1965) *A Comparative Study of the Attitudes to School, Personality Qualities and School Records of Two Groups of Boys in a Secondary Modern School* Unpublished thesis, University of Wales

JONES-DAVIES, D. C. (1968) *A Study of a Social Evaluation System in Terms of a Cluster of Negative Social Attitudes* Unpublished thesis, University of London

JONES-DAVIES, G. A. (1974) *The Integration of Handicapped Children in Ordinary Schools: A Study of the Experience and Attitudes of Headteachers, and the Integration achieved by Five Pupils* Dissertation, Department of Medicine and Dentistry, The University of Birmingham

KATZ, D., and STOTLAND, E. (1959) 'A preliminary statement to a theory of attitude structure and change' in S. Koch *Psychology: A Study of a Science 3* New York: McGraw-Hill

LORENZ, K. (1966) *On Aggression* New York: Harcourt, Brace and World

LOWENSTEIN, L. F. (1975) *Violent and Disruptive Behaviour in Schools* Hemel Hempstead: NAS

NATIONAL ASSOCIATION OF SCHOOLMASTERS (1974) *Discipline in Schools* Hemel Hempstead: NAS

RUSSELL, C., and RUSSELL, W. M. S. (1968) *Violence, Monkeys and Man* London: Macmillan

YOUNGHUSBAND, E., DAVIE, R., BIRCHALL, D., KELLMER PRINGLE, M. L. (1970) *Living with Handicap* London: National Bureau for Cooperation in Child Care

2 Prevention and management

CLIVE JONES-DAVIES

Amongst the many reasons that have been put forward for disruptive behaviour is the increased size of secondary schools that has resulted from reorganization into a system of comprehensive schools. It is often assumed that the very act of expansion precludes the larger schools from providing adequately for the pastoral needs of their pupils. However, I believe that such increases in size may bring benefit in respect to pastoral organization, since the larger schools have consciously to organize for the needs of children within their care. An effective pastoral system can only result from deliberate and well-planned organization of the facilities for supervision and guidance available within a school. The assumption that smaller schools can automatically and spontaneously care for the pastoral needs of their pupils is unjustified, and it is too often the case that children with special requirements are not provided for within such schools because specific responsibility has not been allocated and the staff believe that someone somewhere in the school is undertaking these duties. Some of the following chapters place a particular emphasis on the importance of an effective pastoral system within the school, which may or may not include the services of trained counsellors. An important contribution is made by Derek Poole in his chapter on Education in Personal Relationships: he stresses the corporate responsibility of the staff for the children in their care.

The EPR (education in personal relationships) system advocates the training of some of a school's staff in the principles of educational guidance and care and that other members of staff, although they themselves may not be trained, should be made aware of such principles. Some of the responsibility for the increase in disruptive behaviour must be directed towards those who have emphasized the didactic function of schools at the expense of their pastoral and even therapeutic functions. The chapters of this book which discuss counselling and guidance of children may help to redress the balance between these functions where imbalance exists.

A school cannot however be self-sufficient in its pastoral provision, since other agencies outside school have important contributions to make. The insularity of some schools in dealing with their problems is regrettable, although poor communication and failure to understand the respective responsibilities of organizations do make it difficult for schools fully to utilize existing services. The experience of special schools is relevant here: there is a much greater degree of cooperation between agencies dealing with the problems of individual children in special schools than in ordinary schools. Similarly, communication between departments is much more efficient about handicapped pupils than about the intermittent problems of disruptive children. Although examples of lack of cooperation and breakdowns in communication may be quoted in special education, procedures for informing departments and for bringing into operation their services do exist and achieve the desired results in the majority of cases. A later chapter, by John Stroud, discusses in greater detail the contribution of those services that have relevance for the problems of disruptive children.

When communication and cooperation are achieved, certain important advantages are gained. One of these, one which is all too infrequently attempted in secondary schools, is the compilation of an 'at risk' register. Children likely to cause problems in schools are almost certainly known to such people as social workers, education welfare officers, probation officers, school medical officers and educational psychologists as well as to the staff of the primary schools which they attended prior to their admission to secondary school. An 'at risk' register does not merely identify such children but involves a clear statement of their particular difficulties and needs, thus giving their teachers advance warning of the particular provisions to be made for them.

Another important advantage of clear communication and good cooperation accrues when children with adjustment difficulties who are likely to cause disruption have to be placed in the right secondary schools. A small, but nevertheless real, part of the current difficulties of secondary schools is caused by the admission of children who were attending Community Homes when they are returned for what are called 'home trials' or when they are discharged on the grounds that the therapeutic benefit of the Homes has been fully utilized. Heads of secondary schools are very often faced with the sudden admission of such children with little or no information about their needs and with hardly any time to prepare for the special arrangements that are almost invariably necessary. An improved system of communication and cooperation, between the social services and the education and probation services for instance, would help enormously in such cases. The introduction of children from Community Homes to ordinary schools is an extremely difficult exercise, since the régimes in the two institutions differ considerably. Although the educational facilities of Community Homes may be lacking in many respects, their staffs are experienced and often trained in the management of groups of delinquent and anti-social children. The class groups in such establishments are also, of course, much smaller than those in conventional secondary schools. Furthermore, a different system of sanctions applies in Community Homes, and since such establishments are residential the staff can bring considerably more influence to bear upon children and can in particular establish effective personal relationships. Chapter 9, by Ben Flaherty, shows the problems with which Community Homes are faced as well as demonstrating techniques of management of teaching groups composed of children with a potentiality for extreme disruption and motivated by anti-social attitudes.

The line between prevention and management is a thin one, and naturally the agencies involved in the prevention of disruption are often those most effective in the management of indiscipline. Social workers, probation officers and other extra-education personnel should be involved wherever possible in the school's efforts to manage and overcome their disruptive problems. Other personnel, such as the Education Authority's psychologists, the Area Health Authority's school medical officers and psychiatrists within the area's child guidance service, have an especially important role to play. Though the majority of children causing indiscipline in school might not normally be referred to child guidance clinics, this does not preclude the use of the clinic, for the local psychiatrist will be a specialist in the management of deviant behaviour and his contribution to the in-service training of teachers and his informal advice on individual cases can be invaluable. Educational psychologists and school medical officers are increasingly working in cooperation with one another in schools to counsel children and to advise staff on the management of both disturbed and disturbing children.

A model arrangement, though one which is necessary only in the absence of a school counsellor, is for regular meetings for which the head teacher and his staff prepare a list of children to be discussed and inform the educational psychologist and the medical officer in advance of the meeting. Parents of the child concerned should also be invited to attend, having been informed of the school's intention to involve the specialist staff. The educational psychologist and the school medical officer can consequently come armed with whatever reports and notes on the children are available in their departments. It may be advisable for the health visitor and a social worker to attend the meetings and that they too should be informed in advance of the children to be discussed.

The first hour or so can therefore be spent discussing the children and deciding whether the educational psychologist or the medical officer should undertake the counselling of a particular child, depending on the nature of the problem posed by the child. Each then sees the children allocated to him and also involves the parents, either separately or with the child, in the counselling.

Techniques of behaviour modification lie within the skills of educational psychologists, added to which they have experience of teaching and an awareness of the overall problems of a school. They are therefore able to advise not only on the nature of an individual child's problem but also on the measures which might be taken within classes and in the school in general to eliminate the more indisciplined aspects of his behaviour and to establish in their place behaviour which, in addition to being more acceptable to school, would be effective in meeting the child's own needs. The actual process of behaviour modification would, of course, be undertaken with individual children by teachers largely within the normal routines of school.

Behaviour modification means a more systematic and controlled use of the techniques commonly used by teachers to eradicate indiscipline and to establish alternative, more desirable, behaviour. The literature on behaviour modification tends to be unsuitable for the class teacher, but this does not mean that the techniques themselves are inappropriate or incapable of application within the ordinary classroom. The application of theories of learning which have been found effective in modifying the behaviour of 'special' children are precisely the same as those which prove effective with less emotionally or intellectually damaged children. Behaviour modification, however, is not a haphazard undertaking and clearly marked stages have to be identified and prepared for. Educational psychologists are able to distinguish the component elements of the behaviour that needs to be extinguished and can identify those rewards which will enable more desirable behaviour to be established and the pattern of their application. The training of teachers has always included advice on the establishing and maintaining of discipline but this has tended to be unsystematic and reflects more the experience of the tutor than any scientific knowledge about human behaviour. Teacher education should include a greater appreciation of the development of behaviour patterns in children and the acquisition of behaviour modification skills.

Dilution or concentration?

We have discussed so far only those prevention and management measures which do not depend on the drastic restructuring of the child's timetable or the organization of special provision within a school. Some local authorities are currently establishing special units for disruptive children, especially those who have been suspended from attendance at school. This is a solution to the problem of disruptive children which quickly suggests itself; the models for such units are the maladjusted day units which some authorities have already established either within comprehensive schools or as separate guidance units apart from schools for disturbed pupils. Lack of experience of such units means that it is difficult to determine whether they are appropriate and efficient remedies for the disruptive pupil's problem. Whereas separate maladjusted units have been established on sound educational principles, especially with the aim of providing for maladjusted children the benefits of special education without the drawbacks of total segregation into special schools, the needs of disruptive pupils may well be sufficiently unlike those of pathologically disturbed children as to make such provision inappropriate.

The establishment of special units for disruptive pupils has however certain advantages, especially since the disruption of the normal school routine is immediately diminished. The advantages may be described as follows:

1   If the units are established away from schools a child is less likely, at least in the initial stages, to associate attendance at them with schooling.
2   The establishment of such units may make it easier to implement an alternative and more realistic curriculum for disruptive children. The conventional curriculum of normal schools need not be imposed and opportunities for closer involvement with the community at large, by means of community projects (helping certain sections of the population for instance), work experience or community studies will be greater.
3   Such units would make cooperation between the agencies involved with children easier: social workers, probation officers and other supportive individuals could make contact and work more easily with disruptive children in the informal setting of the unit.
4   The units would provide an alternative placement for the child in which he could undertake a cooling-off period.

Despite these advantages, I believe that the function of a unit for disruptive children should differ from that of an adjustment unit for disturbed children. The latter is established and developed specifically to provide a therapeutic environment for the amelioration of emotional problems as well as to contain children whose personality difficulties are so profound that they cannot easily integrate with other children. The most effective of these units are highly selective as to the children whom they admit, and it is unwise to place children with differing problems in one unit in the hope of developing a therapeutic régime so flexible and comprehensive as to benefit all the children admitted. Such units are not containment units or 'sin bins' but have been established to cater for children with well-defined needs for special educational treatment.

I believe, however, that the responsibility for disruptive children must continue to lie with their school and that the emphasis must be on rehabilitation within the school setting. Problems cannot be overcome and a successful adjustment achieved if the child is removed from the environment within which the problem originated. To segregate these children is to accentuate the rejection they already feel, to highlight the incompatibility which they believe exists between themselves and school and to alienate the majority of them even further. Unfortunately, segregated units all too frequently become containment units, and the children placed there receive less rather than more attention and have fewer rather than more facilities.

The majority of disruptive children placed at such units will see them as a soft alternative to attendance at school. The effective management and education of a group of disruptive and indisciplined children will in all probability be beyond the capabilities of even the most skilled teacher. The phenomenon of 'group psychological intoxication' so well described by Redl and Wineman (1957) is likely to be observed frequently and this group mood, which involves a loss of control by the members together, would make teaching impossible.

The alternative to providing separate units is to retain the disruptive child within his normal class but to make special provision for him. This may include a small unit within the school to which the child might be withdrawn for periods of the school day. The crux of the problem is relationships, and the reestablishment of mutual respect and cooperation should be the aim. To achieve this it is clearly necessary that additional staff should be appointed to schools to enable a more generous allocation of staff time to individual children causing or likely to cause disruption. Such extra staff may be specifically appointed to deal only with disruptive children, though, if possible, they should enable a number of teachers to be released to undertake such duties in addition to their teaching responsibilities. Bernard Baxter describes the operation of such a system in chapter 7. A small separate unit could facilitate the education of some of the more disturbing children by allowing them 'time out' of normal classes. Staffed in turn by a number of teachers all of whom would have received some training in dealing with such children, the unit would provide the opportunity for the individualized schemes of work likely to be essential for the majority of the disruptive group. This kind of organization has the supreme advantage of preventing the disruptive element from exercising a group influence. Dilution rather than concentration of the problem is a more effective method of management.

The report of one of the main teachers' unions on indiscipline in school already referred to, unfortunately makes little mention of positive curriculum changes which might help in the reformation of disruptive children. It might well be said that 'its strength is its weakness' since, quite properly in some cases, it takes a very strong line in its description of the problem and its suggested solutions. However, it makes only a brief reference to the inappropriateness of the conventional secondary school curriculum and greater attention to this, an area for which educationists are all responsible, would have adjusted the balance between a punitive and a remedial approach (NAS 1974).

A more realistic and meaningful curriculum would be a most efficient deterrent to indiscipline. For the majority of the non-academic children in our secondary schools, there is a palpable lack of utility and vitality about the curriculum. Henry Morris, quoted by Ree (1974), talked of the pedagogic fallacy, within which he included the failure of schools to instil in pupils a respect for the curriculum based on their sense of its relevance. He argued that schools must capture that element of the apprentice system which motivated the young person throughout his apprenticeship because he could see the benefits ahead and therefore made him a willing partner in the learning process. Many teachers are able to instil this feeling in even the most antipathetic of children, which explains why there is hardly any school in which disruptive pupils are unresponsive to all members of staff. The success of the teaching profession, which through care, insight and concern has saved countless unstable children, must be stressed. The increased awareness of the need to provide for non-examination children should be welcomed, but still greater flexibility is necessary before the potential of the environment to provide opportunities for curriculum extension can be fully utilized.

Despite these provisions for preventing and managing disruptive children, schools still have the ultimate possibility in their hands, that is, suspension of such children from school. By the Articles of Government of the majority of schools head teachers have the power to suspend pupils from attendance when such pupils become unsuited for education in a school. The process of suspension involves the notification of the school's governors, in the case of the secondary schools, or the managers, in the case of the primary schools, and the local Education Authority. What is involved is essentially suspension. The Local Educational Authority is not released from its duty of providing education for the child. Local Education Authorities have recently examined in great detail both the procedures which might be implemented when a child is likely to be suspended by his head teacher and the educational alternatives available to the Authority for a suspended pupil. The priority, of course, is to prevent the deterioration of any case to a stage at which suspension is the only course of action open to the head teacher. In the majority of cases such procedures include close liaison between the school and the child's home and the involvement of parents in influencing and determining the course of action which needs to be taken.

When a child has proved excessively disruptive, a school is likely to invite parents to discuss with teachers, head and governors the problem presented by the child and to enlist their cooperation in preventing further disruption. The possibility of suspension is usually mentioned at this meeting, as a warning to the child and to the parents. In the event of continued indiscipline on the part of the child, head teachers are often now invited to inform their Chief Education Officer who will arrange a meeting of the head teacher, the parents and any other individual involved in the case, such as a social worker or a probation officer, and a member of his staff. In some Authorities the head of another school in the child's neighbourhood attends these meetings, primarily as an observer. It is made clear to parents and the child that if disruptive behaviour continues the child will be suspended from the school. If there is no improvement in behaviour and 'reasonable grounds' exist, then suspension takes place and the child is placed either at the school of the head teacher who attended the meeting or at another school, the head of which has been informed by his colleagues of the problems involved. A child's failure to respond to education in his new school may then cause the Local Education Authority to ask the Director of Social Services to investigate the possibility of action under Section 1 of the Children and Young Persons Act 1969 and to consider making an order under Section 1 (3) of that Act to ensure the child's care or control.

When such an order has been made, the child is either placed in the care of the Local Authority or supervised by them, or he and/or his parents are bound over to ensure his good behaviour. He is then either returned to his second school or sent to another. In rare cases he may be placed in a community home with education on the premises or in a detention centre. This course of action is unlikely to be applied in the case of a maladjusted child; the Authority should make different provisions for such children, including alternative special schools. Thus children who have proved themselves to be unsuitable for education in normal schools but who are not considered maladjusted are considered to be the responsibility of the Social Services department. Although their continued schooling is undertaken in establishments able to exercise greater control over their behaviour and even over their attendance, it is hoped that it can be geared to their needs and will reestablish a less antagonistic and more cooperative attitude to education.

References

NATIONAL ASSOCIATION OF SCHOOLMASTERS (1974) *Discipline in Schools* Hemel Hempstead: NAS

REDL F., and WINEMAN, D. (1957) *The Aggressive Child* New York: The Free Press

REE, H. (1974) *Educator Extraordinary: The Life and Achievement of Henry Morris* London: Longman

3 Piggies in the middle – or 'Who Sir? No, not me Sir'

BRIAN DAVIES
University of London Institute of Education

Euphemismics, about which much of this book is concerned, is the practice of routinely renaming standardly recurring educational problems. It is usually pursued by experts outside the classroom whose freshly altered discoveries tend to filter slowly, if at all, into the art and vocabulary of a necessarily conservative profession. Thus it is hardly likely to be the case that 'the disruptive child' is a term as yet widely found upon staffroom lips. Teachers, of course, every day define and deal with bad behaviour, reluctance or refusal to work, overt disobedience, and so on – and all of their converses. They trade with children daily in terms of those twins of educational virtue, brightness and hard work, and may or may not believe – probably not – that school has much to do with their generation. They certainly know for themselves that those who would keep order of whatever sort must first catch it, that as elsewhere acquisition via inheritance demands least effort and that the facility can prove elusive, experience over time being the only sure ally in the absence of potent first principles.

Even less likely is the availability of reliable research information upon 'disruption', for apart from its mint-freshness as a key concept, the necessary commitment of an education service in any society to the pursuit of the universally good as currently dominantly defined stands in the way of the will to locate and evaluate any nastiness concomitantly generated. Crudely, schools cannot at all easily publicly confess to harbouring non-worthwhile activities, even if those who run them actually know that they are there in the first place. The compulsory character of schooling adds further bite to its universalistic rule-applying nature – education as the great talent-scouring machine sweeps as it beats as it cleans. Any current sociological talk about 'disruption' therefore has to be conceptual and ought to be sceptical. There are some who would argue that there should be no such talk at all for they are so wedded to the power of the social that they fear that talk alone can create it. Their belief is overdrawn rather than incorrect.

It is important, therefore, in this context, that we start from a sufficiently realistic concept of normalcy. It must be broad enough to include the ordinary experience of harassing the weak and underorganized teacher, losses of group memory in the face of teachers' demands to know all and enjoyment of the cabbalistic power of reducing teachers to nicknames or bundles of slanderous characteristics on childrens' part. So agreed, we may then be in a better position to consider as the focus of our worries about 'disruption' the first-former tearing up exercise books, caught in the broken-open stockroom; the public declaration of the nine-year-old that 'she can't teach me nuffin'; or the fifth-former having a day off from truanting at catastrophic cost to class production norms.

The difficulty even at this anecdotal level is of course, as we all know, that school settings are notoriously well-insulated, even – and perhaps most importantly from the point of view of children – at the level of differing classrooms within the same school. One man's disruption may approximate to another's peak teaching experience, most classroom encounters having that much more to do with F-scales than T-groups. A little whisper in assembly here *may* still bring forth swifter and more powerful retribution than studied child obscenity does there. Learning the context differences is no doubt a vital part of the school experience. But boundary sickness (it arises from unconsidered variety thereof rather than surfeit itself) has become a real secondary school infection. It may have unknown primary sources – the conversation between the part-time infant teacher and the five-year-old that went: 'Please miss are we having you again this afternoon?' 'No, it's Mrs Nails after dinner, Why?' 'Oh miss, I don't like her, she's a real hard one' is not apocryphal but the names are changed to protect the innocent. The secondary school first-year who has by the end of the first term experienced setted maths in a régime of high-quality technicism, unstreamed PE in an atmosphere redolent of Stalag 41, Nuffield Science in the hands of a young lady given to much shouting and English with a phenomenologically-inclined friend of Mao is also perfectly likely to be an empirical reality. If he comes uniformly top or bottom he is almost equally likely to survive intact. More middling, it is quite likely that the individual and his fluctuating group will have settled for a hardened dismay about what it's all for – a confusion with varying standards liable to produce a denial of them all. It plays havoc with the work-rate and does much to squash out the enthusiasm borne up from junior school. It may stem as institutional practice from a laudably democratic definition of professional freedom in one hell of a staffroom. Eleven-year-olds, however, cannot notably cope with the educational schism visited upon them in some of its more virulent present forms. They may be the victims of broken schools manned by disruptive staff groups. All change claims its victims.

I do not mean to insinuate here that dismay and disruption are novel features of our school system or that they are in any simple way linked to 'change'. I am however inclined to take seriously the conventional wisdom about size, though more inclined to see behind it something more properly to do with the wild unbalance of the intakes of some of our reorganized secondaries towards the middle and bottom of the ability range. Big schools clearly need to expend a large proportion of their energy in pastoral work which effectively reduces their scale to face-to-face humanity again. Even if the need is fully appreciated, the energy has to be imported from other sectors of the organization, often to their detriment. The staffroom dispute between pastoral and academic interests may have its financial and demarcatory aspects but it is also often an agonizing over a real Catch 22: if a school don't work hard, it needs a lot of looking after and if it takes a lot of looking after, it don't have time to work hard. Sometimes this is strapped on to the ultimate self-sealer: these children can't be expected to work hard because they are deprived/working-class/less able etc. Like violence of the tongue on the football field, brought to perfection in direct ratio to improved and more demanding refereeing in a faster and more knowing game (do they actually hear more?), our least accepting pupils may coexist in schools with the most dedicated and expert of pastoral men. Someone has said all this before about psychiatrists and mental illness but my point is that even if Canute had had a Ph D. in oceanography he would still have got his feet wet by sitting where he did.

The general point is this: good or bad behaviour by pupils, acceptingness or non-acceptingness, 'disruption' (whatever it or its converse is) exist always in relation to a given state of affairs. As Milton Yinger was at pains to point out (Yinger 1965) a category such as 'deviance', or deviant activity as he preferred to say, can only be understood properly if we accept that it is produced by an individual (with an identity/personality/biography) in precipitating circumstances. To this we can add that those circumstances will be embedded in a social context populated by others with differential access to the power to adjudicate upon legitimacy, though tending to share common assumptions about its core (Matza 1964). We know in sociological terms that deviance inheres not essentially in either the qualities of the act or the actor but in the process of definition by legitimately empowered others. We know that the enforcement of many sorts of deviant labels is highly socially selective, so much so as to make many traditional conceptions of aetiology absurd – though not powerless. However, this discovery seems to have forced the premature abandonment of the idea that even if deviance is processual, some personalities and some social circumstances are more predisposing to being at the 'invitational edge' than others. If the cost of removing all the blame from all deviant shoulders is to render them experience-seeking automata and all enforcement agencies witting agents of the bourgeois state, it is a price clearly too high to pay.

The roots of non-acceptingness or its variant 'disruption' are likely then to be lodged neither entirely in children and their 'background' nor in school and its organizational and curricular arrangements, nor in society in its wider economic, political and cultural aspects, but in all *three* as they interact upon and shape one another. How we apportion blame or determine responsibility is commonly partly a function of our position and interests as well as the precise phenomena requiring analysis. Truth is not easy, but equally the teacher-bashing literature of recent years is surely as insensitive and partial as the perjorations of Working Paper 27 or Boyson being the plain man's Bantock. What they all share as an integral part of their explanation is a monolithic 'working class' and an over-psychologized and determinist view of 'values' as phenomena inhering in social classes. The mainstream and measured sociological view has long been that value differences between social classes largely explain educational success and failure (given a few bits and pieces about intelligence) because of their differential appropriateness to school. Values determine action, and therefore the activity of many children is doomed to failure, negative labelling, poor self image – the 'explanation' runs naturally on – bad behaviour and, presumably for some, disruptive activity. Most of our currently competing educational doctrines could not dispense with this picture, though they apportion the moral turpitude differentially. Marxist images of schooling as bourgeois or state ideological apparatus show expected convergence with those that see it in acknowledged functional terms as meritocratically-leavened behavioural hoops, except that the working class is cast as fateful or feckless respectively. In both cases it loses, for the foreseeable future at any rate. Even away from the ideological extremes the image of school as a 'monolith of middle-class personnel' is highly pervasive. Matched up with an over-romanticized and even archaic image of *the* working class's history, beliefs and life style, the shadows are substantial and satisfying. Teachers may do well to believe in a continuingly *ad hoc* and individual apportionment of the reasons for child success and failure, for in so far as they accept most of what academics have to offer they would lock themselves into paralysing curricular guilt in the face of a predestined clientele. Most parents want their children to do well in an extended school career until school itself tells them that this is not possible (did you believe that Plowden showed that?); the majority of children going to grammar schools since the war have been working class in origin (yes – predominantly 'upper' working class, not in full proportion to their Registrar General share of the population, varying with the percentage of places in a given local authority); Basil Bernstein never proved that *the* working class uses *the* restricted code (the research design wouldn't permit the inference anyway, the essential point about the code is its context specificity, that the five-year-old going to school isn't someone who cannot 'spikadalingo' but more importantly someone who may not be able to recognize the teacher's régime of appeals and control); where teachers and or parents rather than IQ tests have control over secondary transfer, the social bias in the allocation of 'superior' school places increases (perhaps the only thing to mend a bad test is a better test if the enemy is privilege, for the test though biased is blind). One is not trying here to provide a catalogue of educational exotica but rather to show that educators regularly mythologize the appalling complexity with which they are faced. Perhaps they have to in the political/administrative and resource circumstances of education, in order to keep the show on the road. However, to understand is not to excuse and the simplistics of belief in the existence of *a* working class, interests needle-sharp and drawn waiting fecklessly for the bludgeon of over-intellectualized middle-class norms, wielded by class-warring teachers, are evident. What a shame that Marx, in order to make man whole, first had to make him extremely boring.

Hardly less boring, or potentially unreliable – though of undoubted importance – is the violence debate in education. Those who have noted the resurgence of the quantity theory of money in economics now wonder whether it has its educational analogue, such that

$$V = \frac{T \times P}{M}$$

where V is overall school violence, T is teacher violence, P is pupil violence and M is the rate of media presentation in a given time-period. Most people in education seem quite sure that pupil to teacher and pupil to pupil violence rates are on the increase. Even the most pacific of our teacher organizations reports a growing incidence of physical assault upon their members. Others, of course, survey it as avidly as evangelists hunt down sin, while the annotation of teacher violence is left in the hands of equally strongly committed anti-groups. The usual strictures about the reliability of 'official' statistics, therefore, need redoubling here, so that, for instance, the usefulness of the 1971–72 LEA survey by the DES reporting 1,486 pupil-pupil incidents (in 13 per cent of schools) and 313 pupil attacks on teachers (5.1 per cent of schools) remains in doubt until we know more about how events of this sort move from commission to category. This isn't to say, however, that they do not occur at all. Just as with truancy, its gentle brother in the disruption family (in school anyway), we do not know with any exactness whether belief in the incidence is rising faster than the incidence itself. Between the gleeful Jeremiahs and the DES January 1974 survey, truth may rest with the chairman of the education welfare officers' 1973 conference, who estimated nearly half a million daily truants pre-ROSLA. Even in terms of the DES survey, 14.1 per cent of the fifteen-year-olds were absent on the 17th, 4.8 per cent without legitimate reason. The difficulties of various sorts in establishing conceptual and numerical accuracy as to truancy are well covered in Turner's symposium (Turner 1974). From our point of view, we can certainly conclude that awareness of and publicity for teacher and pupil violence have increased dramatically. But whether schools are altogether more violent places requires a balancing of teacher-against pupil-originated violence which we lack sufficient information to strike. Presumably, it is reasonable to assume that violence offered by teachers to pupils is, overall, declining. But an important number of secondaries may be places where overt physical threat by pupils has become commonplace. Frequently what may rescue this is the election to absent themselves by many, particularly older, children. Certain categories of teacher absentee rates in some of our secondaries would also, one suspects, provide interesting evidence of how the safety-valves work.

What on earth can the sociologist say of relevance that might stand the heat of present passions? Carl Werthman, who is in no doubt as to whose side he is on, touches a point of sufficient generality to be worth expanding in this context (Werthman 1963): that the conferral of legitimacy of authority by the pupils is related to seeing that the teacher exercises it on suitable grounds. The 'delinquents' of his study evaluated this on criteria which took into account the area in which the teacher claimed operating rights, his mode of exercising the authority and the way in which grades were awarded (the study took place in a us high school). The same sorts of insights are offered by Geer, who, having defined teaching as inherently conflict-prone (given the built-in knowledge inequality of the teacher-taught relation), distinguishes rule areas within which pupils and teachers would expect one another to have full jurisdiction and 'grey' zones in between, where claims to legitimate influence are in dispute (Geer 1968). These could be viewed as shifting over time, in terms of both internal and external pressures, but never entirely dissipating.

That these ideas touch some vital educational nerves is evidenced by the fact that most authentic educational liberationists have of late suggested solving such problems by abolishing them. A tempting but naive remedy to legitimacy problems is to elevate all possible social definitions to equal legitimacy (Young 1974). This may help to explain the guilty runaway into the magic of phenomenological epistemology recently evident. This in its turn has often been thoroughly confused in its implications by certain protagonists with Marxist species of social engineering which requires prefacing by radical simplification of the story of its possibility. All this has much to do with disruption, for where there is more than one truth capable of exciting belief disruption in the non-trivial sense is always possible. In this sense, it presupposes a social state of affairs which carries within itself a sense of its own usualness or legitimacy consciously under threat or questioning on the part of some of its participants. Properly, disruption involves the deliberate attempt to halt or alter the course of an existing legitimated order. It is interruption with malice aforethought. It proceeds from schism. It is offered by someone who wants to deny or alter how it is.

Much of what happens in schools by way of bad behaviour, from the teachers' point of view, is clearly not disruption in this non-trivial sense. Any social setting will exhibit a rich variety of ruled-wrong behaviour, where far from offering it as threat to the existing social order its producers will themselves acknowledge its badness or shortcomings. Most school misdemeanour, awkward and undesirable though it might be, is of this sort. Although in some schools there may be much disruption, globally one suspects that it remains a thoroughly minority sport. Among those who do not actively embrace their education, our system tends to excite dull compliance rather than active revolt – 'Too many at present seem to sit through lessons with information and exhortation washing over them and leaving too little deposit. Too many appeared to be bored and apathetic in schools . . . [they] don't see the point of what they are asked to do, they are conscious of making little progress' (Newsom Report 1963). If they are entertaining disruption (in common with their more successful school brethren) then as with most socially risky enterprises they are keeping it under their caps. The 'non-acceptance' of the many pupils in our schools who are firmly directed over the invitational edges of low ability/lazy pupil careers does not by any means always lead to disruption. Indeed it has long been pointed out and evidenced (Turner 1973 and the ensuing tradition) that there are powerful forces at work within our system which force the early acceptance upon children of the propriety and inevitability of their educational fate.

And yet there is a pervasive conviction that change is afoot in these matters. If there is truth in this then its possible sources might be either general or local. In one general sense, Waller's intuition still stands – that schools are 'museums of virtue' (Waller 1932) and we can add that their despotism is in even more perilous equilibrium. Authority relations in our society have been changing in ways which those who focus monomindedly on 'productive' relations prefer to underplay. At the most basic and school-relevant level they have changed within families of all sorts in the direction of more egalitarian, guilt-regulated, person-oriented control régimes of one intensity or another. Schools have changed, but possibly neither as far or as fast. This is not deliberately to caricature the complexity of these movements or indeed to deny the economic circumstances at their base. The social origins and functions of 'invisible pedagogy' (Bernstein 1975) have yet to be empirically explored, but it may well prove to be the case that it exacts real penalty from *some* (usually) working-class children who lack the iron of boundary which normally lurks beneath the superficies of most middle- and much working-class fluidity in socialization. Children are never innocent of what is demanded elsewhere and the full-gospel of teacher knows best is being modified forcibly by its trained disbelievers. The legitimacy of the sir-world is under potential threat (though even in the direst of circumstances some sirs continue to get through). Who threatens is likely to be crucially related to children's perceptions of what school is offering them in instrumental terms. Palpably, it offers very differing things both in terms of external vocation and internal esteem.

The major influence upon this has been rightly located in the nature of the occupational system for which school prepares children. That system and preparation for it are both diverse and invidiously ranked. We may only undiversify the system by substantial withdrawal from technological modes, though we may delay in some degree diversification in preparation for it. Some societies have successfully reduced the degree of invidious ranking, though none has yet managed to achieve that without massive knowledge abolition and redefinition. Where there is more than one available conception of social legitimacy, resolution of the ensuing conflict can be via physical repression, therapy, appropriation of the means of knowing, or rationally-based negotiation. For instance, the potentially explosive discontent of those in our schools commonly called 'remedial' is routinely managed via therapy – a strong emphasis on 'personal relationships', meaning teacher manipulation of personal knowledge and affect as a lever for both learning and order. The staffroom wisdom recognizes the category of children not bright enough to create trouble but is often maximally hard-pressed to cope with the one above but not high enough to be full contenders for exam and job success. This group is often successively and viciously sorted out by streaming/setting procedures over the first three years of school life. They are often joined by children riddled down through the school's bad-behaviour rather than 'academic' grid. The educands thus created are not only those from whom the positive virtues of school have been taken away but are frequently those who have been deeply hurt by it and its ineptitude. They may have become equally suspicious of intrinsicalist or instrumental blandishments and pile in their discontent to ordinary phenomena like lateness, modes of address and demeanour. As classroom groups they are often well down the slippery interactive slope with many teachers toward permanent offence and punishment. There is hardly a rule that has not been triply enforced or which has not been brought into contempt. They cannot be trusted with anything (Gouldner 1954).

In schools where many pupils fail to see the point of their education, in a society where traditional legitimacies are publicly challenged, it cannot be surprising that the means of their successful renegotiation are unavailable or atrophied and disruption assumes usualness. To mention cases is itself to risk opprobrium – but violence is daily advertised as political solution in relation to Northern Ireland and other issues; the offensive and protective strategies of the wage- and salary-earner are much more highly developed, for instance voluntary paid absenteeism is no longer a white-collar or managerial prerogative; the right to expect well-packaged and entertaining information presentation has been universalized via the mass media; and older no longer means wiser or better.

School is very much society's creature and, as Cocking points out, part of society's recent change has been to render support for schools more conditional (Cocking 1973). One does not need to be a teacher–right–or–wrong person to see that the effect of this is directly to increase the chance that schools will therapize in order to survive. For Turner, this pops out as a necessity first to tranquillize teacher with the peace of social science (Turner 1973). Fine – who indeed despises a palliative? But if the side-effects contain the crazy decision that knowledge is some sort of general anaesthetic for rendering the working class and black clienteles falsely conscious, let's ask the physician what it is he's been sniffing all the while.

References

BECKER. H. S. (1953) Becoming a marihuana user *American Journal of Sociology* 59, 41–58, reprinted in B. R. Cosin, *et al* (eds) (1971)

BERNSTEIN, B. (1975) 'Class and pedagogy: visible and invisible' in *Class Codes and Control Vol 3* London: Routledge and Kegan Paul

COCKING, R. (1973) 'School and Society' in Turner, B. (ed.) (1973)

COSIN, B. R. *et al* (eds) (1971) *School and Society* London: Routledge and Kegan Paul

GEER, B. (1968) 'Teaching' in Sills, D. L. (ed.) *Int. Encyc. Soc. Sciences* New York: Free Press 15, 560–5, reprinted in B. R. Cosin, *et al* (eds.) (1971)

GOULDNER, J. (1954) *Patterns of Industrial Democracy* New York: Free Press

HOLLY, D. (ed.) (1974) *Education or Domination? A Critical Look at Educational Problems Today* London: Arrow Books

MATZA, D. (1964) *Delinquency and Drift* New York: Whey

MINISTRY OF EDUCATION (1963) *Half our Future* (Newsom Report) London: HMSO

REIMER, E. (1971) *School is Dead* Harmondsworth: Penguin

TURNER, B. (ed.)(1973) *Discipline in Schools* London: Ward Lock Educational

TURNER, B. (1973) 'Pride and prejudice' in B. Turner (ed.) (1973)

TURNER, B. (ed.) (1974) *Truancy* London: Ward Lock Educational

TURNER, R. (1971) 'Sponsored and contest mobility and the school system' in E. Hopper (ed.) *Readings in the Theory of Educational Systems* London: Hutchinson

WALLER, S. (1932) *The Sociology of Teaching* New York: Wiley

WERTHMAN, C. (1963) Delinquents in schools: a test for the legitimacy of authority *Berkeley Journal of Sociology* 8, 1, 39–60 reprinted in B. R. Cosin, *et al* (eds) (1971)

YINGER, J. M. (1965) *Toward a Field Theory of Behaviour* New York: McGraw Hill

YOUNG, M. F. D. (1974) Notes for a sociology of science education *Studies in Science Education*

4 The middle years

MARILYN NICKSON and KEN CHARLES
Greneway Middle School

There is little difficulty in finding support for the argument that the middle years of schooling represent a crucial period in the continuum of child development. It may even be argued by some that the concept of the middle school presents the ideal context and optimum conditions in which to meet the particular personal needs of children of this age-range. Certainly there are many features characterizing the middle years of schooling that demand a degree of attention that might otherwise be difficult to focus adequately on the kind of social problems in particular which these young people are beginning to face. Since we are concerned here with disruptive children in such a setting it may be useful briefly to describe the school upon which this experience is based.

Our school opened in 1969, drawing its pupils from a rural town community consisting of people employed locally in commerce and light industry; some commute to jobs in London and other points south and a fair proportion come from villages in the surrounding rural area. More recently part of our intake has come from a small GLC overspill housing estate. There are now approximately 670 pupils nine to thirteen years of age with the equivalent of 34.5 full-time members of staff. From the beginning, the ethos of the school has emphasized the importance of personal relationships and the belief that intellectual development is best achieved in an atmosphere of inter-personal harmony and respect. The ideas of friendliness and respect are pursued throughout the whole of the school community and involve all adults and pupils alike. Such a philosophy has logical implications for all facets of school life, three of which stand out particularly. First, it demands that we should know our children as well as possible, which means close links with their earlier schools and with parents. Secondly, it requires the participation of a staff who share this particular outlook with all the professional demands it entails. Finally, it also means the adoption of a curriculum with relevant content, one which will bring the teacher away from the desk and in amongst the children in a way which epitomizes the cooperative attitude of staff and pupils. These, then, are three areas which emerge as particularly vital in achieving our selected aims; their importance is heightened when considered with respect to coping with problems presented by disruptive children.

Contact with first schools and parents

Close contact with first schools provides the opportunity to obtain immediate information about children who are either already disruptive or have the kind of problem that makes them likely to become so. It is at this stage that we begin to compile a profile of these children. Visits to the schools are made and personal contact is established with both the teachers and the pupils, thus enabling us to identify problems at the earliest possible time. We are made aware at the outset, then, of the probable demands in terms of special attention that will arise once the children come to us.

The problems in this phase of schooling are more often than not a result of some specific form of learning difficulty, though social deprivation in one form or another also begins to manifest itself in terms of child behaviour. Clearly this can be circular, social deprivation being responsible for learning problems, though learning problems can obviously be inherent in the child, whether deprived or not. The identification of specific learning problems and planning strategies to overcome them may be the easier of the two to deal with. Deprivation, like disruptiveness itself, is relative, and this can make it very difficult to pinpoint. The superficial affluence in which many children are raised nowadays can provide a front for the most severe deprivation of an emotional kind which may form a far more deep-rooted basis for behavioural disturbance. Much of our experience has led us to believe that disruptiveness in school is no prerogative of children from any one social class. By coming to know the children to some degree at least before they enter our school, we may begin to establish the kind of profile that can be most helpful in coping with future problems. In order to extend our preliminary mutual contact a little more, prospective pupils are also given the opportunity to spend time with us before the end of the last term at their first school.

At the same time, parental involvement begins. Once children have been allocated to us, but before they enter the school, their parents are invited to attend an evening session with us and in the course of this dialogue both participants have a chance to gain first impressions of the other. This may be dismissed by some as being too superficial to be of any value, but we would argue strongly that many early insights provided by this meeting have been invaluable in later contact with both children and parents. For example, anti-authoritarian attitudes on the part of parents themselves are often exhibited in such a situation and the seeds of disruptiveness in children may be all too evident from a parental stance of this type. The mother who herself failed to succeed at school and who bears strong grudges stemming from unhappy memories may well choose to take it out on the system now that her own child has entered it. The subtle and not-so-subtle ways in which this attitude manifests itself are many, ranging from a general condemnation of the curriculum the school provides to a criticism of school uniform. It is certainly not unknown for such criticisms to be made by parents within this category even before the child has entered the school.

As well as the advantage of gaining first impressions, it also seems that parents are often willing to talk more freely about their children when they are younger. Therefore the earlier this dialogue begins, the better. The reasons for this may be fairly complex, but one obvious one suggests itself – that the parents at this stage still feel that they exercise more complete control over the child. Later, however, as the child matures and begins to form his or her own opinions, accompanied inevitably by a more critical attitude towards parents, parents may feel this control dwindling and with it confidence in dealing with their children. A certain inhibition in talking about them results. However, by talking freely with teacher in the early stages of school life an openness is established which will scarcely ever be closed and certainly not during the crucial middle years. It is, in a sense, a situation of 'they know that we know' and parents therefore recognize that there is little point in pretending about or disguising certain facts that may later come to affect their child's behaviour in school, particularly if it degenerates into the disruptive kind.

Once the children are with us, parental involvement continues and develops in the normal course of events through personal interviews with form teachers and curricular interviews with all staff who teach each child in different subject areas. A pattern of relationships and background knowledge emerges and is gradually built up. This combination of early liaison with previous schools and with parents is clearly vital to understanding the behavioural profile of disruptive children, in particular as it emerges and provides clues to the causes. To be in a position to identify negative attitudes on the part of both pupils and parents is a very great advantage as the child enters the formative and highly volatile middle years. The knowledge must be used positively, of course, and this depends upon its availability to all teaching staff with whom these children come in contact.

Staff involvement
The organization and running of a school based on the ideals of good personal relationships and respect is a very demanding exercise. Not least of these demands is a commitment by members of staff to these ideals, and the area in which this commitment endures its greatest strain is probably in dealing with disruptive pupils. Therefore, in order to ensure that members of staff are as fully aware as possible of the kind of involvement entailed, a great deal of time is spent in selecting new colleagues. Each candidate is given the opportunity to see the school in action so that they may judge their own potential to contribute to, and gain satisfaction from, the life of the school. The appraisal of course, is two-way. The fact that our approach is extremely demanding is not disguised and it is made clear from the outset that discipline is not enforced by a rigid list of sanctions but largely by reason and example. Thus the staff ultimately chosen are well aware that even in dealing with the most difficult pupils teachers will not have access to some of the more traditional forms of punishment. Clearly strong

support is necessary for staff to implement this approach and this, to a large degree, is built into the organizational structure of the school.

Children within the setting we provide will be entering their third year by the time they are eleven years old. Although the school is organized on a year group basis, specialist teachers largely concerned with teaching their subject in years three and four come to know many children in the earlier years through their work as specialist advisers to years one and two. In this way each child will be known well by at the very least one member of staff by the time he or she is eleven. At this stage the form teacher has an overriding responsibility for the guidance of each child in all aspects of his or her development within the school. Realistically, however, one cannot expect that every child will strike up a strong and close relationship with the form teacher. This may be particularly so in the case of the disruptive child since the form teacher will be the most consistent disciplinarian, and this may, of course, cause a degree of alienation. Therefore every opportunity is sought to encourage the formation of relationships with other staff members whether in or out of the classroom situation. The opportunities in the classroom arise with each subject taught while the out-of-class situation may develop in the context of club activities, sport, or working in the library, on the farm unit or in the school bank. Thus by eleven years of age our children's problems will have been identified and certain strategies will already have been worked out to deal with them.

The depth of knowledge contributed to the profile of each child as a result of regular meetings involving year groups' staff and curricular teams is considerable. Certainly by the third year the cause of problems peculiar to each child will very often have emerged. These may be a broken home with the resultant emotional stress, or emotional stress for a variety of other reasons or other factors, perhaps such extreme opposites as parental lack of interest or parental overanxiety. We rely on weekly contact with social agents outside the school such as the health visitor and the educational welfare officer to give us further help in establishing the reasons for disruptive behaviour. Often they may supply details which help to explain why the child's behaviour takes the form it does, for disruptiveness need not necessarily take an aggressive form. Very often it may simply manifest itself in non-cooperation or, in more extreme cases, in truancy when nuisance-value is equally effective. Whatever its form, it is clearly very important for teachers to be aware of the complexity of causes so that they can approach the problem in as effective a manner as possible. For this reason, all members of staff have free access to all school records and to any information held concerning home background. These records include the normal half-termly curricular records, termly records concerned with various aspects of each pupil's development and behaviour, and records of what transpires in the course of normal parent interviews. In the case of the child with particular problems, records may also include those from a psychologist, a social welfare officer or any other outside agency, as well as records of any special interviews held with parents.

While it may not be normal in all schools for staff to have free access to such information, it is our belief that only in this way can they fully exercise the pastoral side of their role that we consider to be so vital. Clearly the degree of professionalism that this demands of individual teachers is considerable. In our approach we quite consciously adopt the view that every teacher, at least potentially, is also a counsellor. If any one teacher experiences difficulty in following through this approach when dealing with a problem child, there is a chain of referral which may be adopted. First of all the form teacher is involved and, if necessary, the year teacher, a deputy head or the headmaster, depending on the gravity of the situation or the lack of progress made. Whatever the situation, the form and year teachers are always consulted at some point since it is more than likely that they know the child best and will necessarily be involved in any follow-up work. The kind of action staff have recourse to ranges from a reprimand, which takes place in the fairly serious atmosphere of an office, through detention, placing a child on report, work at home detention, withdrawal from class and involvement of parents. Placing on report is usually extreme enough treatment in most cases of disruptive behaviour and has its desired, salutary, effect probably because so many staff, including senior members, are involved.

It may be that the burden placed on probationers and younger members of staff in following such procedures is rather heavy. However, senior colleagues are openly available to share any strain they may experience. In fact part of the duties of the year master or mistress is to keep a special eye out for younger teachers associated with their particular years and to anticipate just such moments of strain. Such guidance and support is another aspect of the professionalism expected from senior members, and the point is made to staff generally that to ask for such support is neither to admit defeat nor to show weakness.

The curriculum – 'hidden' and 'real'

Early in this chapter we described the curriculum as one of three areas highly important to our consideration of the disruptive child. It was suggested that teaching methods which bring the teacher alongside the pupils should be used, not only because they can be an effective way of teaching but because they again exemplify cooperative effort. Clearly both the 'hidden' aspects of the curriculum, that is, its general organizational pattern within the school, and the 'real' curriculum, the content and method of teaching, have a particular impact in dealing with disruptive children.

A particular problem which develops in middle years is increasingly early maturation, especially of girls, and the anomaly arises whereby pupils who are physically young women are taught in an environment which includes male peers who are, on the whole, still very much young boys. The obvious areas of antagonism are school uniform, the use of make-up and demands for privileges of various kinds. Usually it is a few individuals who cause this kind of trouble by flagrantly overstepping the line, and our tendency is to treat each case individually. A fair amount of concentration upon one pupil from many sides – form teacher, year teacher and so on, involving parents if necessary – often brings the desired result and seems preferable to issuing ultimatums to the school at large. Our policy in such matters, as indeed in other areas of behavioural problems, is to try to bring about corrective action but at the same time to divert the attention of the girls or boys to other matters. This is usually done by enlisting their help in undertaking different responsibilities, for example library duty, caring for animals on the school farm or possibly helping with the supervision of younger children during 'wet breaks'. More recently a school council has been established and, while it cannot be claimed that characteristically disruptive children are members of it, they certainly use it to voice their protests. That their views or complaints are taken seriously and discussed takes the heat out of the situation and lessens much of the adverse effect their behaviour might otherwise have had.

We end by referring briefly to the 'real' curriculum – the more formal part of teaching and learning – because we are very aware of the dangers inherent in our particular approach. With the emphasis upon harmony and respect and the resultant heavy pastoral demands on teachers, it can be all too easy to sacrifice the formal aspects of the curriculum to the pursuit of inter-personal ideals. Even the most disruptive pupil deserves, and often will demand, to be taught something. A balance both from the pupil's and the teacher's point of view must be sought. For the pupils, this means content which is or can be made relevant and which will equip them well for the next phase of their education and beyond. For the teacher to attempt to do this and to individualize the process at the same time is clearly a difficult task under the most favourable circumstances. To attempt it with pupils who have behavioural problems because of a variety of causes is even more challenging. While we claim a fair degree of success in coping with our disruptive pupils in this way, we are realistic enough to admit that we are not achieving total cures. Disruptive behaviour will no doubt surface strongly again in many pupils in the upper school years. Evidence from the upper school suggests, however, that at the very least this is delayed for a considerable time and if in that time another firm relationship with a member of staff can be formed then much of the battle is won.

In the most extreme cases probably all we as teachers may ever do is to perform a kind of 'holding action' with respect to these young people and their basically anti-social behaviour. It is, however, beyond question a very worthwhile experience to attempt to reach them through the medium of personal relationships and, in the case of some at least, we hope, fundamentally to change their attitudes.

5 Disruptive children in school—the view of a class teacher and head of house

KAY PARRY
Brockworth Comprehensive School

The observations made in this chapter are based on the writer's experience in a rural seven-form entry comprehensive school in Gloucestershire, although it is probable that they are generally true of schools in both urban and rural areas.

A disruptive child is a child who, knowingly or unknowingly, effectively and frequently disrupts his own education and the education of others. Fortunately the percentage of seriously disruptive children in a school is usually small (about 5), but unfortunately just one chronically disruptive child can damage the education of a great number of children. The amount of time needed and taken to deal with a disruptive child in the classroom can effectively interrupt and undermine the education of other children.

To be faced by such a situation is the classic dilemma of a teacher. He or she has to decide whether to deal with the individual at the expense of the others or to remove the individual for the good of the whole. In many circumstances the solution is clear and the problem can be dealt with quickly and completely. But sometimes the solution is unclear and if the disruption becomes repetitive or tumultuous then the removal of the source of the problem becomes essential. A surgeon usually decides to remove a simple canker from an otherwise healthy body. Once removed the canker can be disposed of and the body returns to its healthy state. A disruptive child is the canker of the classroom. But here the similarity ends. The disruptive child obviously has many problems and needs help. Without individual therapy in depth, the child is not helped, just hindered, and the associated problems are not solved, but often compounded. It follows too that the earlier the surgery the greater the chances of successful treatment and a complete recovery. The earlier a child's problems are recognized and treated, the greater is the chance of solving them, before they become a fixed part of the youngster's personality.

Recognizing the problem

Disruptive children do not appear to have the same backgrounds or the same problems, though their pattern of behaviour is similar. These children need help and the disruptions they cause are cries for help.

Part of a child's education is to learn how to become an active and helpful member of society. This is achieved primarily by contact with small sections of society, for example the family or the school. If a child cannot establish relationships with other people or has difficulty in placing himself within the community, then it falls on the other members of the community to guide and help the child. If the child feels insecure at home, or the family is unable to give the necessary help, then it becomes the school's task to help the child to solve its problems and become a responsible person able to cope with the difficulties of day to day life. In recent years, more as a result of circumstances than design, the mantle of social responsibility has fallen heavily upon the school, which now finds itself growing into a principal social as well as educative agency. While the school has always accepted a certain social responsibility, it is now under increasing pressure to accept a greater responsibility and is inadequately equipped to deal with the depth and variety of these problems, particularly the breakdown in family life.

There is some evidence to suggest that, in cases of soccer hooliganism and vandalism to property for instance, the child causing most problems in society is also the disruptive child in school. It is also probable that the present increase in disruptive and aggressive behaviour in society is reflected within schools. Though this aspect of the problem is beyond the scope of the present chapter, two other contributing factors should be mentioned here.

1 ROSLA

Any large-scale alteration in the life of a school will cause disruptions. The raising of the school leaving age was generally welcomed but unfortunately it brought unexpected as well as expected problems.

Some children are bored with school by the age of fourteen and object to being contained within the system. School must be made meaningful to these children, and they need to be highly motivated. Unless they are, they will increasingly disrupt their own education as well as that of their peers. Also these pupils often assume that they are young adults and object to being treated like schoolchildren. Their education must be seen to be alive and to be directly related to daily life. Attempts have been made to achieve this, but generally the facilities required to cope with the needs and demands of these pupils are not available. The unsuitability of the courses offered to these pupils results in increasing boredom and eventually causes disruptive behaviour first from the dissatisfied and unmotivated individual and ultimately from a whole group of dissatisfied pupils. More practical courses are needed, and these demand money.

2 Drink

Drink is a drug and can alter the mood and personality of the individual. Drinking amongst the young is causing increasing concern among educationists and children as young as eleven have shown evidence of drunkenness during school hours.

Drink is socially acceptable and since children ape their elders as well as their peers it is becoming more common to find youngsters drinking. Children still at school who see drink as a symbol of maturity are frequent and sometimes heavy drinkers; fourteen-year-olds have been known to return to school in the afternoon in a drunken state. Their resulting behaviour is extremely and immediately disruptive: a drunkard is difficult to handle at any time, but in front of a class of fourteen-year-olds the situation is difficult in the extreme. This is a problem new to schools and one which can only be dealt with in the short term by having the child returned to his home and his parents informed. It is also essential to discover the source of the drink; once this has been located the shop-manager, publican or even parent (if it has come from the home) must be informed. A confidential discussion with the relevant party usually has the required results.

Pupils who drink in the evenings often suffer the repercussions in school the next morning. A hangover is not conducive to a learning situation!

Easy access to drink is one of the roots of the problem. This can be quickly and simply remedied by closing loopholes in the laws governing the sale of drink; for instance drink should not be displayed on open shelves in supermarkets. At peak sales times it is difficult and often impossible to ascertain the age of a youngster.

The glamour of drinking, fostered by advertisements, is another attraction to youngsters. Advertising should work both ways and emphasize the dangers as well as the glamour of drink. Schools have an urgent and important role to play in stressing these dangers and should regard it as an essential part of their social education programme.

The actual problem

In large schools, cries for help can pass unrecognized until a peak has been reached resulting in frequent disruptive behaviour. At secondary school level, the child can pass from classroom to classroom and teacher to teacher in a tense, highly emotional state eventually erupting into disruptive and aggressive behaviour and causing havoc.

Thus it is essential to have within large schools a tight and close support and contact system to ensure that such behaviour is recognized early and over the whole spectrum. An early-warning system for the child and the teacher can cushion the force of the disruption and protect the education of the other children as well as help the individual.

Every child needs to feel the security of a smaller unit within the large. Thus a large school should be subdivided into smaller units, a microcosm of the whole. The division of a school into a house or year grouping gives the child a close feeling of identity and can facilitate communication. In either case the child will find it easier to identify first within a tutor group and then within his house or year grouping.

43

In theory such a system is good, but in practice it can fail. Very often the particular teacher who has special contact with a child is teaching and cannot deal with the situation as it happens. Delay can mean that the problem is contained but not solved.

To cover this contingency there must also be someone within a school available at any given time to concentrate on such a problem as it arises. This does not necessarily mean one person on permanent duty, but a group of experienced teachers one of whom is always on duty.

Suggested support system

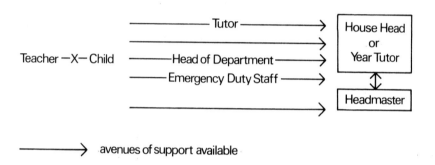

To have the time to delve deeper into the problem and to analyze and solve the problem at source is also important. The person dealing with the problem should not just be a 'container' or a 'holder' but an 'adviser', a 'solver' and 'initiator of help'.

Finally, close liaison and discussion between the relevant staff is important at all times, as roles often overlap, and consistency of approach in dealing with a problem is vital. For example, the teacher coping with a disruptive child might ask for help from his head of department, who may deal effectively with the situation. Whatever the result, the incident must be reported to the child's tutor or house head as the child may be causing problems in more than one subject, and a number of people may be trying to deal with the same problem in different ways. This can have serious repercussions. Communication must work both ways, the house head or year tutor also informing the staff of any changes that might affect a child, for instance separation of parents.

Tackling the problem
Once disruptive behaviour has been recognized, an instant dialogue between the parents and the school is necessary. First the parents are

invited to the school to discuss the situation by letter or by telephone. It is sometimes necessary to visit the home; a blind parent or a parent suffering from a heart condition may have difficulty in organizing a visit to the school without the help of others. Some parents are simply frightened by the size of the school and are happier with a home visit. Too often the parents of disruptive children are themselves inadequate and do not understand the problem: the mother who cannot read, or whose husband is away, and whose numerous younger children take up all her time and energy needs special consideration.

In most instances, the offer to help a child is gratefully received by parents. Once agreement has been reached, help can be instigated. On occasions parents are afraid to acknowledge or refuse to accept that a problem exists. Delicate handling is needed at this point but when eventually the parents realize that the school is offering to help not to punish the child they will agree to cooperate.

It is often necessary to provide a special type of therapy for the whole family, not just the child. This requires the help of outside agencies including educational welfare officers, social services, the school medical officer, the educational psychologist service, the police and the local doctor.

Friendly and fairly regular contact with outside agencies on an informal basis is advisable. If help is then required quick contact can be made. Too often an impersonal 'phone call does not have the necessary speedy results. Many schools today establish active, informal contacts with these agencies. These are necessary since a school plays an active part in the daily life of a large section of the community: it is the drawing-board of the future generation and can pass on as well as assimilate the general trends in society.

Coordinating meetings with all possible contact agencies on a regular basis can in the end pay dividends. General discussion of recent changes and developments, for example of new laws governing child employment, new developments in the social services, can give a clearer picture of the wider trends, and information gleaned can be stored for future reference. At the same time a particular problem can be discussed with the relevant social worker in a friendly informal atmosphere. When an emergency then arises instant contact in depth can be established and specialized advice sought. Such meetings held at least once a term, when representatives of outside agencies are invited to lunch at the school, are very rewarding. The visitors and relevant staff mingle informally over a buffet lunch, and the opportunity to discuss particular cases with specific agencies is a welcome procedure. After lunch the discussion usually becomes more formal; perhaps the chief probation officer has been asked to speak about the reorganization and range of his service and how contact might be made. The headmaster might speak about the organization and problems of the school, and in particular to specify where help is needed.

Thus whenever disruptive, irrational behaviour occurs on a fairly regular basis a broad pattern of methods and techniques can be evolved.

The first stage occurs within the school. The teacher dealing with the disruptive child attempts to place the problem by identifying the child's behaviour trends and patterns. Discussion with the child and the parents then follows. The collection of information should be as swift as possible, for the time factor is very important. Also a pleasant room for talking to the child and the parents is a basic requirement that is often lacking. Once information has been received and the problem discussed with the child's parents, the teacher makes an assessment. If the help of an outside agency is considered necessary then it must be obtained as soon as possible. Since many outside agencies are overworked and stretched to the limit they cannot react quickly; in this case the problem has to be handled as far as possible within the school, often with limited success.

Common cases of disruption

Although the causes of disruptive behaviour vary, we may identify some recurring patterns of disruption.

The classical disrupter

The child lacking in attention and security will use every ploy within his grasp to get the attention he is seeking. Self-discipline has never been encouraged in the child; no one has cared enough to reward good behaviour. Attention to such a child is often seen as a reward for bad behaviour rather than punishment. Therefore the bad behaviour increases in the hope that the amount of attention will increase. There comes a time when the child's claim for attention has to be thwarted, and often an emotional storm results. The child has no idea how to limit or control its outburst.

The obvious answer to such a problem is to give the child the attention it seeks, but in a controlled, secure situation in which he will eventually learn to solve his own problem. But no school can afford the ideal ratio of one teacher to one child. The actual remedy therefore has to be a compromise. The child needs and demands more attention than the normal classroom situation can provide. A closer, family-type situation is needed. To exclude or isolate the child or to place him in a remedial group when his problem is emotional rather than one of inability to learn only aggravates the problem.

The child needs closer contact with smaller groups in a stable environment if his emotional needs are to be catered for and eventually solved. A small specialized unit within the school to deal with such children would be appropriate, but few schools have such a facility.

Within the unit the child will meet other children with similar problems. Handled carefully, they could learn to help each other. The smaller grouping gives the teacher more time for each child, and this closer supervision and care might encourage the child to gain the confidence and determination to overcome his problems. But during this process the

46

child's general education is interrupted and he may find it difficult to reintegrate. To overcome this difficulty the child can be gradually eased back into the system, step by step, lesson by lesson. A logical method would be to reintroduce the child to one subject he liked and one he disliked, to see if he could now cope with the latter as successfully as with the former.

At the same time outside agencies should visit the home to ensure that the rest of the family as well as the child are receiving the support they need. If the child needs specialized help, i.e. child guidance, it is often advisable for that help to be given in school, where the child is beginning to feel secure. Also the local Youth Leader might encourage and support the child by persuading him to take part in an activity outside the school, perhaps joining the Youth Club and becoming a member of a games team.

The intelligent disrupter

Some children not only wish to lead but also to dominate. They are capable of organizing and directing other children who bow to their superior force. These are natural leaders but their potential is misdirected. They often dominate at home and are self-centred, but they are clever enough to manipulate their classmates without their realizing it. Once they have learnt how to dominate the other children the next step is to test the dominance of the teacher. This often takes the form of a takeover bid. At first the child will offer assistance and be most cooperative. Gradually the relationship grows and starts to alter subtly, and suddenly the teacher may find himself being taken over and organized. If the signs have not been recognized early enough, or if the child fails to respond to a quiet chat, a head-on clash will result and the child will be publicly chastised. The loss of face will be deeply resented by the child and the atmosphere in the classroom will change swiftly. The child will try to manipulate the others and will openly challenge the teacher's authority. Male teachers often find older girls difficult to deal with in such a situation. Similarly older boys will often resent a female teacher telling them what to do. Blatant disruption by older children must be dealt with immediately and, if necessary, severely at a high level before the situation gets out of control.

Such a situation often develops because the child is bored rather than emotionally disturbed. Suitable courses with a high interest and participation level are necessary to motivate the child. For example facilities at the local technical college might be explored with the aim of sending groups of children for half a day per week to a 'mini' mechanical engineering course, a photography course, a hairdressing or catering course.

The truanter

Disruption by absence can also upset the relationship between pupils and the teacher. The constant truanter can effectively disturb the classroom situation. When the teacher asks another member of the group for an absence note, the pupil will fairly reply – 'Why pick on me, Jane's only been here twice this term, why don't you do something about her?'

Obviously something is being done, the usual welfare officer visits, talks with the parents. When these fail it is necessary to accumulate evidence over a long period of time (about a year) before prosecuting the parents. Meanwhile the child loses a valuable amount of schooling. When eventually the case reaches the court a £5 to £10 fine seems ludicrous in comparison with the effect the lack of schooling will have on the child's life.

What is more, the other children's cry of lack of fairness is partly justified. Justice has taken too long and is not effective. This often results in a spate of petty truancy which overburdens an already over-extended system.

Thus, the sanctions taken to protect the majority from the erring individuals fail to be effective in the eyes of the majority and are most difficult to justify. Cries of 'double standards' and 'unfairness' are hard to refute.

It would be more useful if the punishment fitted the crime and the court ordered the child to attend recognized units set up specially for habitual truants.

The unintentional disrupter

A child with physical and mental handicaps often displays odd rather than disruptive behaviour. But such behaviour can effectively disturb other children. Some children will use such a child as bait to cause disruptions. A child that has difficulty in coordinating body movements – one which for example takes fifteen minutes to put on a bathing hat or ten minutes to do up a shoe lace – can become the brunt of children's often vicious humour. This calls for strict and immediate intervention on the part of the teacher.

Children with physical handicaps obviously need specialized medical attention. Some of these handicaps are hard to recognize but can effectively disrupt a child's learning. Partial deafness can account for the persistently loud, talkative child who appears to ignore instructions. Thus regular medical inspections are important. The perceptive teacher usually notices the various signs, and most schools have fairly frequent and efficient medical supervision.

The petty criminal

Some children steal to obtain what they would otherwise never have, others steal to claim attention, others to buy friendship and a few for the excitement. When a child steals regularly and is seldom caught, the excitement seems worth the almost negligible risk. Successful larceny makes the child bolder and the crimes increase in volume and size. This has a dual effect on other children. Some children see the apparent success of the offender and will eventually try it for themselves. This is borne out by the marked increase in shoplifting among children of school age. Offenders often offer part of the haul to other children who thus knowingly or unknowingly become accessories.

One known thief stole £20 and distributed it among his classmates in proportion to his feelings of friendship towards them. The others knew the money was stolen yet accepted it, and not one child reported the incident, which only came to light when the police caught the culprit and informed the school. The threat of swift vengeance either from the thief or from the receivers who profited from the theft was enough to prevent its disclosure.

The school's role in dealing with such situations is difficult. If a child is found to possess stolen goods in school then the police should be informed immediately. But the situation is frequently not that clear. The teacher often hears rumours and has suspicions but no concrete evidence. Yet the teacher has to try to protect the rest of the children. The growth in the number of children involved in stealing, however petty the crime, is alarming. It appears to be prevalent amongst all types of children, not just the insecure, more and more of whom seem to enjoy the challenge involved, the headiness of success apparently outweighing their pangs of conscience. The police are very willing to come into school and talk to the children, and this can be a useful procedure. But, the young offender once detected is not often effectively punished in the courts. As in the case of the child who persistently truants, the boy who steals regularly and is eventually caught and only cautioned appears to have survived virtually unscathed. Even a second offence involving larger crimes simply results in a supervision order for a few years. This is not an effective deterrent and the punishment appears inadequate. Many children assume the criminal has not been punished and therefore cannot have committed a crime. This often results in an increase rather than a decrease in juvenile crime.

The advent of supermarkets and larger open-plan stores has made temptation greater for a vulnerable child. Also, many large stores are averse to prosecuting children. The petty thief must be more effectively deterred so that he does not become a hardened criminal.

Disruptions by girls

Although for girls as for boys adolescence is a stage of development in which they seek to achieve greater independence, girls are generally less extreme in their reluctance to comply with authority. Consequently the problems they pose for schools differ somewhat from those which result from the natural aggressiveness of adolescent boys. The disruption caused by girls stems mainly from emotional difficulties which are the result of unfavourable circumstances and experiences and they are generally more amenable to the guidance of teachers. However, cases of extreme disruption can occur, and because these have an intense emotional undertone they are often difficult to manage and sometimes impossible to resolve. Furthermore the censures available are fewer and there is a tendency on the part of teachers not to be so severe with girls as with boys.

The following are three cases of girls who were of considerable concern in school.

49

Case A Marjorie

Marjorie entered the school at the age of thirteen, when the family moved into the area. At the time of writing Marjorie is sixteen years old and will leave school at Easter 1975.

Home background

Marjorie's mother is separated from her father whom Marjorie seldom sees. Her mother is in her mid-thirties and often displays unstable, neurotic and occasionally hysterical behaviour. She has a history of mental illness. The home is obsessively spic and span. Marjorie's younger brother, Frank, is epileptic and prone to violent fits of temper accompanied by heavy breathing and a marked change in features.

The mother places a great weight of responsibility on Marjorie. For many years she withheld her love from her and there have been violent scenes in which the child was told to get out and later prevented from leaving. Marjorie has 'slept out' on several occasions following family rows. Quite paradoxically the mother has confided in Marjorie, taking her out drinking, and then left her to go home while she goes out with Uncle Tom. Uncle Tom is at present living with the family: there have been a succession of 'uncles'.

Marjorie's relationship with the opposite sex are not yet mature. She has been heard to say that she cannot stand anyone to touch her or be near her. This is probably because she witnessed a great deal of her mother's activities too early in life. Whilst she plays an active part in the social life of the village, as a person she remains aloof. She is an elected member of the committee of the local Youth Club and plays games for the club; yet she has little real social interchange with her peers. Much like an infant, she still plays 'alongside' but not 'with' people.

Behaviour at school

It is common to see Marjorie walking about during lessons. Often she appears to be walking purposefully and yet she is only seeking to avoid arriving anywhere. If stopped, she may run and consequently provoke staff to a 'confrontation'. A great deal of her time in school is spent in a moody or disturbed condition. Her mannerisms are directly related to her mood which, sadly, is often a black one. When obviously upset or disturbed she averts her eyes from those present, tossing her head and pursing her lips. She becomes flushed and studiously ignores all attempts to converse either by going into a corner and facing the wall or by suddenly dashing away. If ignored whilst in this frame of mind, she will suddenly shout out, or if she is near a wall, blackboard, table or desk she will write her name in a large quick hand. Marjorie has been seen to climb into cupboards and to 'hide' from staff in the presence of full tutor groups, thus creating a major diversion. She has danced, clambered, swung, dodged and leaped about to the great amusement of other children watching. Whilst she can have quite long periods of lucid behaviour her mood can change very quickly. Even her physical features alter during a tantrum, so much that staff have remarked that 'she looked a different person'.

Marjorie is extremely unpredictable with respect to routine times, places or events. She is late for registration and frequently misses it. She truants internally and hides away in odd corners, often with a cigarette.

Her lessons are in hopeless disarray so that her entry into a group has to be negotiated on an individual basis. Every attempt has been made to encourage her involvement and her interests, yet she still refuses to attend lessons which do not interest or entertain her. Marjorie's associates in school appear to be either younger children or those 'in trouble'.

Action taken

Marjorie was seen by the county educational psychologist about six months after her arrival at the school. He discussed the child's management with the head of house and advised the involvement of the family's doctor to whom she was referred a few months later. Following consultation with the school the doctor agreed to see her and report. He indicated that he was aware of the family situation and emphasized that there was little practical help he could give to the school.

Meanwhile constructive help was offered at school. Marjorie showed an interest in helping older people and the school made arrangements for her to visit regularly the local senior citizens' home in conjunction with her school project. Marjorie became very involved and enjoyed this commitment but she soon started to take advantage of it and often left school at unscheduled times, missing lessons.

The situation was discussed with Marjorie but she continued to cut lessons. Although a wide choice of subjects of interest had been made available to her she failed to cooperate. Eventually sanctions were introduced which resulted in her suspension. She returned with a letter of apology which was accepted by the headmaster.

When she was readmitted Marjorie was very antagonistic. Her time-keeping has improved but she has made little effort to converse or participate socially. She still cannot communicate her plans and is again suspected of truanting. At present she is fairly subdued but exists in a state of unsympathetic isolation.

Conclusion

Marjorie will leave school at Easter 1975. There is little doubt that the school has had to deal with an extremely disturbed and antagonistic child through the difficult phase of adolescence.

If Marjorie's problems had been diagnosed and a referral made when she was younger, a special school might have helped her. Whilst we have offered considerable help in terms of time spent with her, regrettably little or no progress has been made during the last year. Cooperation from Marjorie has been entirely lacking. There is a possibility that she might find employment working with old people but this might not be wise on a long-term basis.

Case B Shirley

Shirley is now fifteen years old and throughout her school career she has shown an inability or unwillingness to conform to acceptable standards of behaviour.

Home background

Shirley is the third of four children. The youngest boy is a cousin and was adopted as a baby when Shirley was five years old. Her mother is highly-strung but quite sensible and concerned; she tends to favour her elder daughter and son. Shirley is very jealous of this and competes for her mother's attention. The father is extrovert and easy-going; he does not understand Shirley and tends to tease her and joke at her rather than with her. Shirley finds it difficult to listen to or respect men.

Behaviour in school

Shirley has shown disruptive tendencies since her first days at infant school. While at junior school her parents were advised to take her to a child guidance clinic. An appointment was made which Shirley and her mother attended. Her mother greatly objected to some of the questions asked and adamantly refused to return or to accept any other help. This was a great mistake, as at this stage significant help could have been given and progress made.

Shirley's entry into secondary school was unfortunate; a superficial report was insufficient to indicate her problems. The group she was placed in included (as later events showed) other disturbed children. Martha, another member of the form, showed a strong, demanding personality and had definite leadership qualities which had been misdirected. Arthur came from one of the inadequate families of the community and showed a marked lack of knowledge of, or respect for, many standards.

These three spent the first year trying to gain attention. Shirley had a number of petty tantrums which usually took the form of screaming, uncontrollable behaviour lasting for a few minutes. Each member of staff teaching Shirley was warned of the potential danger and was advised to send for the relevant house head immediately. On most occasions these disruptions necessitated Shirley's removal from the classroom. This was followed by a quiet, calming but serious talk, which ended with Shirley bursting into tears of remorse.

Towards the end of Shirley's first year at school her parents were invited to the school to discuss the problem. Her mother came and admitted awareness and concern for the problem. The same behaviour was experienced at home. The mother was willing to discuss and involve herself with the school to help to sort the problem out, thus reversing her previous attitude. It was suggested that she should visit an educational psychologist and this time both parents agreed. Shirley started to meet the educational psychologist on her regular monthly visits to school. She enjoyed these chats but the effect on her classroom behaviour was not marked.

By the end of the second year Shirley's behaviour had again deteriorated. Martha had by this time asserted herself, becoming Shirley's friend and manipulating her as she wished. Both girls protected and mothered Arthur. These three dominated and controlled the behaviour of their group; disruptions increased within the classroom. The situation demanded positive action, Martha was obviously the leader and after much discussion with teachers and parents, Martha was placed in another group.

Inexperienced teachers found this group difficult to handle so the third-year timetable for the group was consciously set to ensure that the group had experienced teachers. These two manoeuvres solved the problem for the group as a whole. But Shirley continued to have uncontrolled outbursts which decreased in number but not in intensity. Removal from lessons and 'talking around' sessions were still necessary but were rarely to be effective.

After a multiple outburst, tactics were changed and Shirley was suspended. As requested the parents visited the school and volunteered to keep Shirley home for a week in the hope that their shocked and ashamed attitude, plus time away from her friends, might make her aware of the seriousness of the situation. This proved effective for a while.

Shirley is now in the fourth year. Her subjects were specifically chosen after thorough discussion with her parents and herself. Shirley has always enjoyed the company of younger children, often in preference to that of her friends or family, and she wishes to work eventually in a children's nursery. Shirley was therefore encouraged to follow a child-care course and a course specializing in establishing relationships with others. These subjects are taught in small groups and have a practical bias; Shirley can identify more easily within these groups. The courses entail regular out-of-school visits, particularly to a local children's play-group. Shirley enjoys these visits and is aware that her outbursts would make her liable to have her privileges withdrawn.

Conclusion
Shirley is beginning to understand the depth of her problem; she will never be able to control it fully but she is learning to cope with it. Her outbursts are less frequent now that she has become more involved and interested in school.

During her first three years at secondary school, Shirley needed more attention than it was possible to provide. An hour of calm in the same stable environment at the beginning of each school day would have given her the balance she desperately needed. If the referral recommended by the junior school had succeeded her problems might have been erased before they became an integral part of her personality.

Case C Mary
Mary is a third-year pupil who enjoys school.

Home background
Mary's parents are divorced, her mother has remarried and she has a step-brother. At the age of five Mary witnessed the tragic death of her younger sister, about whom she frequently talks. Her parents were divorced soon after this incident. Mary has refused to accept her step-father and still sees her father quite frequently. Her step-father has tried to build up a relationship with her but she has refused to listen to or accept his offers of help. Frequent and intense quarrels are common. The atmosphere at home is strained. The mother deals with the situation as best she can

Mary had attended the child guidance clinic for a number of years before she entered secondary school. The educational psychologist was deeply involved with the family and arranged for Mary to indulge her passion for dancing, entering her for and taking her to competitions during the weekends.

However when Mary was preparing to enter secondary school relationships within the home again deteriorated. The mother was finding it difficult to cope. At this point Mary was offered a place at boarding school, but the mother decided to keep Mary for another year to see if the situation might change.

Behaviour in school
Mary was a small but determined child when she entered secondary school. Fortunately the move suited her. Two major factors contributed to this change: her tutor group was pleasant and stable with a sensible and sympathetic woman tutor. Mary still has difficulty in establishing relationships with men.

Mary displayed a few minor tantrums during her first year but her eagerness to please and sympathetic handling by staff soon smoothed these outbursts over. Since then her adjustment and development in secondary school has been pleasing.

On only one occasion has a serious disruption occurred. Mary's tutor group has a good standard of behaviour and is very sociable. Mary has integrated well within the group and is most helpful and reliable in carrying out small duties.

However outside school Mary still has problems. The family situation is still difficult and Mary's questioning of her step-father's authority still continues. Mary is frightened of her step-father and displays her anger and frustration on the community. In the last year she has been cautioned for shoplifting and is waiting to appear in court for making a hoax-bomb call.

School is the stabilizing factor in Mary's life at present. Help came at an early enough stage for her to establish relationships outside the family. She has been fortunate in her relationships with adults in school since, unlike her step-father, the staff have exercised their authority wisely and have gained cooperation from Mary. Her behaviour in school is a product of this stable relationship and it may be assumed that in its absence Mary would have shown signs of the same anti-social behaviour that she manifests out of school.

6 Coping in the school situation

ANNE JONES
Headmistress, Vauxhall Manor School

Teachers are understandably ambivalent about the disruptive pupil, alternately angry and despairing, rejecting and self-denigrating. Nothing divides staffrooms more effectively into two camps than a discussion of how to deal with deviants. Whilst so much emotional polarization is engendered, it is difficult to look rationally at the problem and almost impossible to do anything about it. Few people deny that there *is* a problem – except those who hope that by so doing it will go away. Some people pander to the problem, indulging in psychological and socio-economic excuse-making and wallowing in a sense of being overwhelmed and impotent. Few really come to grips with what is happening and do something about it.

This is not surprising in an age when schools are very confused about what they are trying to do. It is unfashionable to be authoritarian, rigid, controlling, directive or judgmental. In swinging away from these polarized extremes, in attempting to be child-centred, consumer-orientated, flexible, democratic, non-directive and non-judgmental, we may at times be falling into yet another trap, that of seeming to be without a sense of direction, without powers of judgment, without authority, without anything to teach. Some of our pupils are disruptive because they do not see the point of school: they do not see the point of school because neither their teachers, nor their parents, nor society are really sure what the aims of education should be in this very complex and rapidly changing era.

In thinking and talking about the 'disruptive pupil', teachers, parents and the public at large are prone to exaggerate the size of the problem. The media, the local grapevine and the natural desire of the teacher to tell a good tale about the blackboard jungle, all play a part in feeding our fears and fantasies. So the first task for any school which is serious about coping constructively with its disruptive pupils is to find out, as rationally and objectively as possible, the extent, the nature and the cause of the problems. You would think from reading the papers that whole schools were full of professional lesson-wreckers, yet in each class there may be only a minute proportion of disrupters, admittedly very often wielding undue influence on their classmates.

Attempts to quantify the extent of the problem remain relatively few. Professor Rutter's study of children in the Isle of Wight showed an overall deviance rate of 10.6 per cent, though not all these pupils were disruptive (Graham and Rutter 1968). A similar study which he carried out in an Inner London borough showed a deviance rate of 19.1 per cent. The ILEA Literacy Survey (1971) showed a rate of 21.6 per cent for boys, 16.3 per cent for girls. My own research in a London secondary school, also using Rutter's social adjustment scale, showed a deviance rate of 24 per cent among first year pupils. However, 37 per cent of these were classified as neurotic and on the whole were not disruptive, if anything rather introverted and withdrawn. Many of this group could best be helped through counselling. Of the rest, labelled 'antisocial', most were not, when systematically assessed and discussed, either delinquent or in need of psychiatric help. They behaved badly at times not because they were totally depraved or deprived but for other simple and rational reasons. Maybe they found the change from primary to secondary school too bewildering; maybe they were experiencing difficulties in reading and writing which led to feelings of frustration and aggression; they had too much physical energy and not enough space to let off steam; they had missed out on various socializing factors – they had not learnt to wait their turn or control themselves; sometimes they were over-controlled at home and broke loose at school; sometimes they were bored, got no sense of achievement out of their work; sometimes they had a weak teacher who did not stimulate or stretch them sufficiently.

These are all problems, real problems, but they are not insoluble. Many can be tackled quite systematically by a series of strategies designed to work at these specific points. What we must not forget is that disruptive children, like teachers and parents, come in many different kinds, each of which may need different handling. Blanket treatment, a polarized, rigid solution, will help only a few. To be effective, diagnosis and treatment need individual assessment. Before we come on to discuss the various strategies which may be used to help the disruptive child and (just as vital) the disrupted teacher, it is important to look at different kinds of disturbance. Nearly all have their roots in the home environment, but some may be exacerbated by the way the school handles its pupils.

Referrals to child guidance

The number of grossly disturbed pupils in normal secondary schools remains relatively low. When I was working as a school counsellor, I estimated (on the basis of six years' work) that one or two pupils in every form of thirty would need to see a psychiatrist, that is approximately 5 per cent (Jones 1971). Unfortunately those who exhibit the most gross behaviour problems are rarely those who accept the need for child guidance. On the occasions when a school blackmails them into going for treatment (by threatening expulsion if they don't) these children may not respond to the methods used, unless they are removed to a special school where their problems can be worked on consistently. The physical lesson-wreckers, those who commit violence and outrage against teacher or school property, are by and large not the type to respond to soul-searching. Whilst they may have a need to verbalize the anger which drives them to such outrages, they may not find this easy, even if they are willing; their parents too may be more used to acting out rather than verbalizing their conflicts. Thus an occasional visit to the child guidance clinic will not have a favourable prognosis in many of the cases which teachers find the most upsetting.

In this kind of case there is a need for the development of new techniques, for example behaviour therapy, which may well be best practised where the problems are actually happening, that is, in the classroom. In one area of London, an experiment has been mounted in collaboration with the Institute of Psychiatry to see if ways can be found of helping teachers to deal with serious behavioural problems within the classroom. The project is based on recent American studies which have demonstrated that the way a teacher responds to a difficult child can dramatically affect that child's behaviour. A group of teachers have undertaken a ten-week evening course to enable them to apply these principles in the classroom situation. It is too early yet to evaluate the results, but this appears to be one way of helping the teacher to deal with the more intractable problems as they arise. It is understandable but it is also unfortunate that we so often unconsciously reward and encourage disturbing or attention-seeking behaviour amongst our pupils.

We also fail to refer pupils who do need psychiatric help early enough to specialists. A classic syndrome which I have observed in every school I have ever worked in is when a pupil is allowed to make havoc for several terms, even years; when finally the patience of staff and pupils is exhausted, then the child is referred for child guidance with demands that he should immediately be taken off roll and sent to a special school. When it then transpires that there is a six months waiting list at the child guidance clinic, no room at a special school and that the child's parents won't, in any case, go anywhere near a child guidance clinic, the school wrings its hands in despair and says that the psychological support services are no good. In fact the problem may be that the school has made the referral too late. It is as if the teacher in the classroom is afraid to admit his pupils need help, as if this in some way reflects upon his ability to control his class: when he is desperate enough, he brings in the head of house or year, who also spends a couple of terms trying to prove he is not going to be 'beaten'. In desperation he finally brings in outside helps – by which time the child is well and truly set in a pattern of misbehaviour. The school has colluded with the problem. It should have asked for a specialist opinion right at the beginning: there is no harm in asking, you can only be wrong; there is harm in waiting, for you can leave it too late.

Socio-economic problems

Some of the pupils who disrupt our lessons are not psychiatrically disturbed, but they do live in very disturbing home circumstances, in particular in poor housing, overcrowded and broken homes. There is a growing tendency for teachers to want to do something about this; they may even try to act as agents of political and social change. Many will in any case feel sorry for the pupil with a 'difficult' home background and excuse him his behaviour because of his 'hard life'. There are several fundamental misconceptions here. First there are limits to what a teacher can and should do to change society: it can be useful for the head to write a letter in support of a rehousing claim, or for the school to call a case conference to get some concerted action about a family whose psychological problems may be rooted in their physical living conditions. But feeling sorry for a child does not help him with his difficulties – it may in fact compound them. There may well come into play what I call the 'law of diminishing expectations': 'he can't help it, his family has got problems', 'Officer Klopsky I'm really a slob' as the ingenious song in *West Side Story* puts it. This is a way of handicapping further the have-nots: for he who expecteth nothing shall not be disappointed. It is good that we should try to understand why our pupils behave as they do, but we must remember that children are adept at playing up their weaknesses: rewarded for this skill they only become weaker.

We must also remember that there is not necessarily any correlation between disturbed behaviour in school and social conditions. In my present school a study of truants is currently being undertaken. The factors in their background are being coded and compared with those of a control group of 'normal' pupils. The results will be very interesting whatever they say. All I know from my experience as a counsellor is that many children with absentee or drunken fathers or mothers, with countless brothers and sisters and very little space for living or playing, are splendidly resilient, mature, resourceful and able to cope with the adversities of life in part *because* they have 'difficult' home backgrounds. Many a cossetted close-carpeted darling develops no inner strengths, feels unloved in spite of his material well-being and has just as many problems as his 'poor' relations. So it can be misleading and unhelpful to expect a child to have problems.

Counselling

More real, and more amenable to help in school, are the problems of the child, whatever his background or intelligence, who feels unloved and rejected. His symptoms vary from angry attention-seeking behaviour to pathetic-seeking-after-teacher or withdrawal into mild depression, all of which can be disrupting to the teaching process. This sort of child will respond well to a positive relationship with his teacher, and particularly well to counselling. I will return later to the complexities of establishing a stable and fruitful pupil/form teacher relationship. What the counsellor has to offer the child who feels undervalued is a relationship based on nonpossessive warmth, congruence and genuineness. It is not (or should not be, in my opinion) a kind of 'feeding on demand' relationship, which is what the teacher may be forced to provide and which may not always help the child because it enables him to manipulate adults unduly. A counsellor should be able to offer a regular session which the pupil can rely on as his very own. I found when I worked as a counsellor that many very insecure children grew in strength and confidence simply from having a regular session with me. The fact that I was outside the normal classroom provision meant that I had no axe to grind. My positive regard for the pupil was not conditional on his good behaviour in my class – and so he was able to be himself. By expressing his true feelings and his own doubts about his behaviour, without having me mock, correct or collude with what he said, he seemed to be able to get himself into perspective, to realize that many of his difficulties in relationships came from the way he behaved. When he was angry he could ventilate his angry feelings; when he was sad he could cry, when he was fed up with others he would say so without being told he mustn't say things like that.

Counsellors, like psychiatrists, are not magicians: they cannot achieve the impossible by waving a magic wand. Some children are not suitable for counselling; these will need alternative forms of treatment. As a counsellor I found that approximately one-third of each class I worked with referred themselves for counselling and of these (ten in each class of thirty) usually at least two would be suitable for long-term counselling whilst another two would need referring to specialists. The essence of effective counselling is that the client (in this case the pupil) should *want* to be helped, should accept counselling as a valid way of being helped and should be prepared to work at his problems. Counselling is no easy way out for the lesson-hopper, for the work is done by the pupil, he has to lay his feelings out before himself and examine them. In a nutshell, as in all learning processes, the pupil must be motivated, otherwise the process is a waste of time.

To describe counselling in full here would take too long, but interested readers should pursue further the literature on counselling, including my own account of my work in a girls' comprehensive school (Jones 1970). The system I set up was designed to be preventive rather than remedial and was based on self-referrals as far as possible. The objectives were to help the normal adolescent in school in the following ways:

1   to provide support for a child who was experiencing some unusual situational stress (parents in hospital, new baby in family, death of a relative)
2   to help pupils with developmental problems to do with the onset of puberty (the need to rebel against authority and to establish relationships with the opposite sex)
3   where appropriate, to make referrals to specialists (child guidance, social services, family welfare etc) at the earliest opportunity

4   to improve communication and understanding within and between
     the home, the school, the community and the resources serving that
     community
5   to support and train teachers in their pastoral care functions.

All these strategies were helpful in reducing the numbers of disruptive
children in the school. But even when I was counselling it was patently
clear to me that counselling was only *one* way of helping and in some cases
was a completely inappropriate method.

Remedial teaching

It is extraordinary that one of the most obvious causes of disruption in the
class is the one which the teacher should be equipped above all to deal
with – namely, learning difficulties. In a recent experiment in London
schools, in which ways of helping children with special difficulties were
systematically tried and evaluated, the most clearly consistent success was
in the language development and oracy projects. Admittedly these took
place in primary schools: perhaps the secondary teacher, in spite of the
overwhelming evidence he faces daily that many of his pupils are poor
readers and writers, has not yet adjusted to his remedial role. Many
secondary teachers are alarmed when faced with illiteracy and
innumeracy, claiming to have no training and no skills for coping with
such problems. Yet until the teachers have taught themselves what to do
about this situation, their classes will inevitably be full of disruptions. Until
secondary pupils can read and write, much of what they are taught will
pass them by uncomprehended. No wonder they become restless.

  Whatever the virtues of mixed-ability teaching (and they are many), it is
undeniable that if in fact the ability range is not mixed but grossly skewed
towards the less able, unless the teacher is both skilled and confident he
may fail to satisfy the intellectual needs of all his pupils. The disrupters may
well come from all levels of ability. The bright child may not be stretched
at all and may therefore become bored and restless, the average child may
be under-achieving, aware that he is not dim, yet still not equipped to do
the work of which he is capable and therefore frustrated. The less able child
may be trying to push himself beyond his capabilities; finding the whole
thing too much of a strain, he may well give up and resort to some
disturbing activity which gives him a kind of false prestige as a rebel leader.
I am not claiming that this is a fair and accurate picture of the average
British classroom, but I suspect that most teachers will recognize elements
of what they face daily.

  The answer is not simple, but it is at least one which calls upon teachers
to be teachers, which they are, rather than psychologists, social workers or
therapists, which they are not. It certainly points to the need for more in-
service training for *all* secondary teachers, not just remedial teachers, or
teachers of English. I feel that if teachers addressed themselves primarily to
this problem, which is within their aegis, rather than to socio-economic

and psychological problems, which are not, they might find that they would make surprising gains in terms of confidence, motivation and positive behaviour of their pupils.

Parents
Whilst some of the learning difficulties faced by pupils may relate to the quality and kind of teaching they get, others may be complicated by pressures from home: not just those of the under-caring parent, but also those of the over-concerned and anxious parent, the parent who has unrealistic ambitions for his child, or who is over-protective, unduly controlling or punitive. I find that these problems are often faced by children of immigrants who have come to Britain seeking enhanced prestige and better job opportunities. When they discover that the system, either in society or in schools, is not as simple as all that, they are bitterly disappointed. Their children may find the school all too permissive and undemanding, and the net result may be frustrating for all. On the other hand, the kind of parent who appears to his child not to care at all, to have abdicated all responsibility and authority, equally sets up problems for his child which will be reflected in school. So what does the school do about parents? Ever since the Plowden Report (1967) *et al* so effectively pointed to the importance of parental attitudes to education, teachers have felt burdened with the need to work with parents, as well as with pupils. Plowden was referring to attitudes towards school, but many teachers have gone one step further. Realizing that the parents' attitudes in general need working on, a keen teacher may set off on a home visit, fired with missionary zeal and hoping to change the way parents behave. He may be right in thinking that work with parents on this scale needs to be done, but he is wrong to think that it is his job. Teachers have neither the time nor the training, nor is it their role to undertake family casework. A school which is particularly convinced of the importance of this kind of approach and which feels that even the best efforts of the welfare and social services are not satisfactory would be well advised to appoint a trained teacher/social worker who understands the dynamics and limitations of working with families.

I am not saying that schools should not work with parents. I am a strong supporter of the idea that parents should be involved with the education process as much as possible and at as many levels as possible. But the well-meant efforts of the conscientious form teacher to change parents' behaviour may be misplaced and may misfire. If the teacher concentrates on producing a well-taught pupil, then the parents will have less to worry about in the first place.

The anti-social
If we assume that broadly speaking the neurotic child will be best helped by counselling, this still leaves a large group of anti-social children. They may comprise the under-socialized, the undisciplined and the immature.

One important way of helping them is to improve the teachers' classroom management techniques. Many of these children simply need firmer handling: not more *rigid* handling, but more positive, purposeful and constructive handling. When I was doing my 'Rutter' survey of social adjustment, I was greatly struck by the differences between various classes, differences which undoubtedly related to the way they were taught. Some teachers had almost *no* difficult children: this I thought was very suspicious! Others appeared to have a whole classful of anti-social children, which seemed equally unlikely. Upon further investigation, I found that the teachers who were themselves most unsure and in doubt about what they were trying to do had the greatest degree of classroom disturbance. In other words, children will 'catch' the mood of the teacher. The minority group of unsettled children will behave badly and lead others to behave badly if they sense that the teacher is worried, unsure, in conflict, tense and not sure what to do next! I am not condemning the teacher who feels like this, merely pleading for greater support and training for the teacher in the classroom situation, in particular for the probationer teacher or the 'returner' teacher.

The immature

Those children who are under-socialized and immature will not always respond readily to firm discipline. They may need to be taken back through very simple socialization procedures step by step. It helps if they have the same teacher for much of the time so that they know what to expect and can build up a pattern of positive behaviour with confidence. In many London junior schools in recent years 'nurture' groups have been established in which children are given a kind of 'mothering' in small groups. They are provided with the training, affection, rituals and varied experiences which a mother would normally give her child before the age of five. Cooking, eating, drinking, sharing, going out together, waiting one's turn, cooperating, caring for others: all these experiences provide for the child knowledge of what is expected of him and subsequently a feeling of being a valuable, loved and loving member of a group. As a result he may become more able to cope with the greater stresses of the ordinary classroom situation.

Unfortunately, it seems to me that many of our secondary school children lack 'nurturing' as well and I advocate the provision of similar experience in the secondary school. Many schools do already attempt this through normal teaching procedures, but not with the kind of teacher-ratios and equipment that are necessary for the job to be done effectively. For these under-socialized children, the need is neither for talk nor for chalk but for actual first-hand experience of what, for whatever reason, they missed out on as young children. The immature child must be brought on gradually from the stage *he is at*. It is no good calling him a baby and expecting him to become adult in one short step; he has to be weaned through the various stages. He will be able to go more quickly when he is older, but he will not go overnight. Neither will his emerging new 'mature' behaviour be consistent. He is bound to regress at times and move forward unevenly, but if his progress, however slight, is recognized, he will be encouraged to persevere. If it is not, he will sink back into some childish mode of behaviour because this may be more effective in getting him the attention he craves.

The mature

The problem for some of our disruptive children is not that they are immature but that they are in many respects mature beyond their years. For them the strictures and petty regulations of school life may seem childish: indeed I think we should ask ourselves how often our rules and regulations are childish. I can think of several sixteen-year-olds who out of school lead what I would describe as 'normal' adult lives. One boy had a Saturday job with tremendous responsibility, good money, a chance to take real decisions and to learn from making real mistakes. On a Saturday night he went to the pub and enjoyed himself like many young adults. I can think of a girl who had a baby and returned to school; she looked after her boyfriend and her child, fed them, washed, ironed, shopped, nurtured and loved them in a most responsible manner. Both these young people behaved with great seriousness and achieved efficient success in their out-of-school lives. In school they had to toe the line, follow the dictates of the school bell, only do as they were told: it is not surprising (to me at any rate) that they kicked against this. They did not need to *learn* how to live in society the play-way; they knew they could cope with life after school, in some ways more successfully than the teachers who were struggling to teach them. These are only two examples of what must be an increasingly common problem now that the age of majority and the school leaving age are practically the same. So a school has to ask itself how it will meet the needs of its mature students to be treated as adults. If they are treated like children, they will most certainly rebel and behave childishly; if they don't rebel, then this is also rather disturbing, for it shows an unhealthy degree of passivity.

The socializers

The last category of disruptive pupil is the 'bored' pupil and the 'social club' pupil. These may share many of the characteristics I have already mentioned. These are the pupils who see no point in school as an educational institution. Lessons are boring, or meaningless, or irrelevant, or they've done that before Miss and don't want to know. It is a con to think that simply by making the lessons more relevant they will suddenly be inspired to learn and to work. These are the 'passive' rebels; they became 'switched off' long, long ago. They are usually quite harmless unless you try to make them work too hard – then they will make life difficult, so that in the end the teacher and class may well come to an unspoken truce: provided the teacher does not bother them they will not bother him. They come to school all the time, not to learn, but because it is a warm friendly place where if you play your cards right (and sometimes literally your cards) you can chatter with your friends – quietly – all day long. School in fact is a good social club, much better than hanging about the streets.

This small group of pupils is, I think, as disturbing as the group which actively disrupts. It is disturbing because from it emanates the feeling that it is *not* the done thing to work in lessons. Those who might want to learn are under tremendous pressure from the group not to bother. And so many serious students, unless they are exceptionally strong-minded, or conscientious, may be afraid to do themselves justice for fear of losing their status in the peer group. The teacher faced with this situation has to build up the confidence of the group that wants to work so that in the end it becomes acceptable to work in the lesson. But it is no easy task and the teacher may need extra help in order to do this.

In discussing the various kinds of disturbing pupil (many of which overlap), I have already mentioned many of the practical problems and indicated some ways of dealing with them. The most important point for any school to remember is that adding on ingenious and complicated mechanisms for dealing with misfits will be useless if the main system of the school is not itself as good and consistent as possible. The clearer a school is about what it is trying to do, the more positive will be the response of its pupils, for they will see where they are going to go and what the point of it all is. They will get a much-needed sense of achievement and this in itself will enhance the self-esteem and positive feelings of all. In creating an effective organization in the school, administrators have to watch and make sure the system serves the needs of the pupils. Too often an organization takes on a life of its own, which may well contradict or stultify its stated objectives.

Secondly, it is very important for academic and pastoral objectives to be implemented together, otherwise they may in fact undermine and contradict each other. This 'double message' may be one of the things which turns a pupil off: the school claims to value and trust him and to care about him, yet he may be locked out at break, locked in the playground at lunchtime and may not even be taught by his form teacher.

Secondary schools have a great deal to learn from primary schools about the organization of stable learning groups, with attendant stable teacher/pupil relationships. Do we really have to play musical chairs every thirty-five minutes in secondary schools? Is what we teach our young pupils really so specialized that it must be taught by a specialist? Have we ever been to see how they do it in our feeder primary schools?

A sceptic once remarked that secondary schools appear to be organized in such a way as to prevent pupils and teachers from forming a relationship. What is known fashionably as 'the tyranny of the bell' may simply be a device for disguising poor teaching and poor teacher-pupil relationships. Certainly, the kind of pupils who disrupt our lessons will, by and large, also be those who find it hard to adjust to adults quickly or even to trust a teacher they do not know well. It is noticeable that in London schools new teachers are regarded with suspicion until they have *proved* that they are really sufficiently interested in their pupils to stay more than a year. If teachers spent more time teaching their own form, they would find it easier to establish a relationship of trust with their pupils. Pupils who feel valued, secure and trusted are less likely to want to destroy their class or their teacher.

It is glib, however, to assume that the job of being form teacher is an easy one, for it is not. It is ironic that many schools which put in a form period to allow their form teachers time with their forms find that the form teachers at a loss to know what to do with that time. This may not be an argument for abandoning the idea but rather for training and supporting the form teacher in what is expected of him. This is something we need to do far more systematically. When it is done well, the form teacher is likely to be more effective and less distraught, for he will not be perpetually torn with doubts himself about what his role should be. When the form teacher is relaxed, confident and calm his form is also likely to be more settled.

The form teacher (and consequently his form) is also likely to be more relaxed if he feels well supported by the school's ancillary services. Teachers are still curiously reluctant to let anyone else help them with their job – yet the teacher who is conscientious will find himself overloaded with pastoral follow-up duties, and the teacher who is not will simply ignore what should be followed up. The teacher's prime task is to teach as well as he possibly can; if he is given more ancillary help, either from the clerical staff, or in the classroom, he may find he is able to do his job more effectively, and this in itself will stop his pupils from being so disruptive. If there is a problem at home, then he must get the education welfare officer to visit, not rush round himself. He must know what the services on offer to him are, he must be introduced to the personnel involved, and he must not be afraid to ask for help and advice from the relevant agency.

In my last school, we had the following provision for pastoral care, which we established over three years. First, we ran integrated studies courses in the first two years which meant that form teachers taught their own forms for half the week and really got to know them well. Our first-year pupils were all systematically tested and screened. They were given tests in reading, maths and non-verbal reasoning and then the social adjustment scale; I used the results myself as a basis for discussion with the form teacher. Any children who needed specialist help of whatever kind were referred early.

We appointed two teacher/social workers, one for Lower School and one for Upper School. Their job is to work with heads of year, form teachers and parents, to coordinate the interventions of other agencies, and to make a link between home and school. In Lower School we appointed a counsellor who does group work and individual counselling with all the third years and with younger pupils at their request. In Lower School we set up a school-based tutorial class which fulfilled some of the functions of a nurture group, helping children with behavioural problems to work through their feelings by being taught in a small informal group. Children with learning difficulties are given remedial help on a withdrawal basis. In Upper School a further 'home-base' class was set up to help the children who still had difficulty in following a more academic course: they went to normal lessons as much as possible but were given extra remedial help in their classroom, where they were also allowed to take refuge when they and their lesson were incompatible. Through links with a nearby psychiatric teaching hospital, a group for difficult adolescents run by a psychiatrist was set up. Similarly, a support group for staff was established and met once a month; this supplemented the regular year team meetings. Staff attended voluntarily and a psychiatrist, social worker and psychologist, all from a nearby adolescent unit, were also present. It was the kind of meeting in which nothing was done but much was achieved in terms of mutual understanding and trust. In particular we were able to look at ways in which the school handled pupils and set up certain tensions. New teachers and form teachers were given regular support and training, both through the probationer support scheme and through the heads of year. Contact with parents was encouraged, through interviews at school and particularly through the report afternoons and evenings to which all parents were invited to discuss their child's progress. This proved to be a very positive way of making contact with parents. The net result of all this activity was not that there were no disruptive pupils but that we did at least have a main system and an ancillary system designed to help such pupils as far as possible.

Some of the work we did was a direct result of the 'Children with Special Difficulties' scheme fostered by the ILEA between 1972 and 1975. Under this scheme some six hundred special projects were set up in London schools. Most of the schemes fell into the following categories:

Sanctuaries or withdrawal groups
Nurture groups
Support for teachers
Diagnostic and screening techniques
Opportunities classes
Links between schools
Links between home and school
Language programmes
Projects designed to broaden pupils' experience
Pastoral care and arrangements
Off-site centres for school refusers
Improvement of school environment

Evaluative research into the effects of the 'Children with Special Difficulties' project shows only a marginal improvement in the behaviour and performance of those children who received special help (such as we provide). What is salutary to discover is that the secondary control group, who received no such help and were initially better adjusted, deteriorated over a period of two years to a point on the scale *below* those originally picked out for help. This is not an argument for giving up the 'Special Difficulties' scheme but rather for extending its methods and approaches across the curriculum and to all pupils: for reconciling and working at the affective and the intellectual components in education simultaneously, not separately.

We must do what we can as well as we can. Schools cannot take on the problems of society as a whole without collapsing under an intolerable burden. It is vital that we recognize the limits of what we *can* achieve if we are to continue to work vigorously and confidently. If we take on too much we shall achieve little. We can only do our best within the limits of our task, which is to educate our pupils. If we know what we are trying to do and why, then our disruptive pupils are likely to diminish in number. Given a sense of purpose, of achievement, of stability, of being valued and cared for, they will neither want nor need to disrupt.

References

DES (1967) *Children and their Primary Schools* (Plowden Report) London: HMSO

GRAHAM, P. and RUTTER, M. (1968) *British Journal of Psychiatry* 114, 581

JONES, A. (1970) *School Counselling in Practice* London: Ward Lock Educational

JONES, A. (1971) School counselling *Trends in Education* 23

7 Tackling the disruptive pupil

BERNARD BAXTER
Longbenton High School

There have always been disruptive pupils: I was a member of a country grammar school A stream that drove a gentle physics teacher to distraction, and at the impeccable single-sex school my wife attended girls threw tennis balls at the blackboard when one teacher turned her back and put snails in the desk of another who could be relied upon to flee from the room in consequence. It is true that there was a certain chivalry in these proceedings twenty-five years ago and that today disruption has rawer and more intense connotations. Today's adolescents have acquired and assumed more freedom than we had, kick more strongly against restraints and authorities, observe fewer signposts in a rather more desolate landscape. But they have greater confidence and poise, they have their hands on one of the levers of power, spending capacity – hence massive entertainment and clothing industries devoted to them and their money; their music is vigorous and participatory and their clothes less dull and uniform than ours were. Their parents are at home less and grant them privileges earlier; the media, which will make a story out of anything, have elevated their sillier and more vicious episodes to heroic levels; urban spread has boxed in and devitalized a greatly increased population; there is an ethical and philosophical gap left after the erosion of the old moralities; the older generations appear by turns bewildered, grasping, corrupt and at all times unable to control either present problems or future prospects. In short, it is a difficult age in which to grow up. What has happened has been in effect like one of these percentage pay rises across the board which reward the indolent and the hard-working equally; we have given – and the young have taken – a general increase in freedom which applies equally to the intelligent, the talented, the generous, the creative and to the misguided, the disadvantaged, the potentially criminal.

All these walk in through the school gates, and the school is directly responsible for their education and social training for a remarkably small, if concentrated, proportion of their lives – less than one sixth of any year during their school span. Education sometimes seems to lose credibility in the public view because of exaggerated expectations about what it can or should achieve; at the same time school is one of the dominant agencies in a child's life and its influence extends far beyond the hours of physical attendance. Furthermore, all parents are amateurs at the job of bringing up children, and – despite the potentially enormous advantages of the family group and its covert as well as its overt relationships – it is not surprising if some of them do not manage to do it with conspicuous success.

The trap of dwelling on one part of the picture, such as 'disruption' (or drug-taking, or football hooliganism, or any of the other black terms of our time), is to concentrate too much on the minority; the vast majority of our pupils never develop serious behavioural problems. And I am prepared to claim as an article of faith that no child (apart from a tiny minority of the mentally sick) is irreclaimable, however difficult and irritating he may be. 'Disruption' is a blanket term with emotive overtones: quite a lot of children are sometimes disobedient, rude, abusive; very few are continuously so; very, very few offer serious physical threat. It is true that even a small minority can disrupt out of all proportion to their numbers and consume attention, resources and nervous energy beyond reason; but it is part of the professional function of the skilled teacher to deal effectively with the difficult as well as the cooperative pupil. Teachers of experience know that problems are better played down than inflated, that confrontation is usually unwise because it drives people into positions from which they cannot retreat with self-respect – and then of course they turn and lash out. This is not an argument against firm standards of discipline but for the guidance and understanding which will achieve them. Pupils need status appropriate to their capacity to exercise judgment (always bearing in mind that the older are always too grudging in their estimate of when the younger arrive at this capacity); but they need more than this. One of the professional skills of the teacher is to safeguard pupils' self-esteem when they have worked themselves into positions that endanger it; sensitive adults have always helped children through their experimental years by tactfully (and even at apparent loss of personal face) ensuring their extrication from extreme positions and a route back to normal relationships.

Background

In September 1970 Longbenton was reorganized as a mixed comprehensive high school for the thirteen to eighteen age range based on three secondary modern schools, using the existing buildings of two of them (a boys' and a girls' school on the same site). Its initial clientele was about a thousand pupils continuing from the three schools, and it was not until September 1972 that the full ability range (350 pupils in the year group) transferred from the four middle schools which feed the high school. In 1974–5 the full ability range is in the fifth year, and in September 1976 the members of this year group who are still at school will reach the upper sixth. A little over a third of the fifty-five staff in 1970 consisted of teachers from two of the secondary modern schools who had opted for the high school, the rest being new appointments, sixteen of them probationary teachers. Of the three secondary modern schools two had developed quite strong fifth forms and all were streamed (in one, fourth and fifth year organization was based on 'package deal' courses – o level, commercial and general). The staying-on rate to the fifth year was about 20 per cent. The reorganized structure of education in the area, with first schools (five to nine), middle schools (nine to thirteen) and high school (thirteen to nineteen), was thus very different in philosophy and emphasis from the previous structure of primary, secondary modern and grammar schools. The grammar school transferred premises, pupils and staff to nearby Killingworth New Town to form the basis of another high school in a similar pyramidal structure. In terms of local loyalties Longbenton High School drew together the communities of Longbenton and Forest Hall (on the north-east outskirts of Newcastle-upon-Tyne), between whose youth population strong rivalries had existed in the curiously nurtured terminology of the day, Benton Boot Boys and Forest Hall Aggro. The growth of Killingworth New Town generated new rivalries. Catholic education in the area provides its own primary, secondary modern and grammar school structure.

In the late 1950s the Longbenton estates constituted one of the largest local authority housing provisions in the country (though they have no doubt dropped some way down this dubious numerical league since then), with some high-rise and some three-storey blocks of flats and a majority of semi-detached council houses. Subsequent in-filling has removed most of the original green areas within the estates and the effect of overcrowded humanity is very striking. Forest Hall has a considerable proportion of council housing, while the original village of Benton and Forest Hall and some new areas attached to the latter consist of a sprinkling of owner-occupied properties. Throughout the area recreational facilities are minimal – no theatre, cinema, swimming-pool, dance-hall – and boredom among young people contributes to a plague of graffiti, vandalism and other anti-social behaviour. The very provision of these facilities in the New Town is a cause of some local discontent. Youth centres based on schools and the work of voluntary organizations are very important in the life of young people in the area, as are the school-based adult associations and evening institutes, dances and other social functions run by parent-teacher associations in the life of the community as a whole.

In the first year of the high school's existence there were clearly identifiable short- and long-term problems. In the short-term, in 1970 – 1 there were fourth-year leavers at Easter and summer whose allegiance to the new school was likely to be tenuous, and indeed a hard core drawn from the low streams of the previous schools made difficulties far in excess of their numbers, though this proved to be a 'one-off' non-recurring phenomenon. More generally, the high proportion of pupils from large families, eligible for free school meals, from one-parent families, with fathers unemployed, constituted a problem of deprivation that will always be with the school. Two statements made again and again by mothers visiting the school to talk about their children's problems speak volumes:

'I'm under the doctor for me nerves'; 'Is dad'll kill im'.

We aimed to set up a school with as large a measure of mixed-ability teaching as we could achieve, a strong pastoral support system, a relaxed atmosphere in which friendly relationships and mutual respect could flourish and in which above all individual pupils could develop their particular talents and achieve highly in them. In a sense it is putting things backwards to deal first with the system we devised to tackle the problem of the disruptive pupil and second with the principal features of organization and philosophy within which the system operates, but this order coincides with the conclusions we reached very early at Longbenton, that a healthy social order was the basis and condition of successful education.

The 'rehabilitation' system

When the year's timetable is constructed, each period in the week is 'shadowed' by a teacher who has on that occasion no other assigned class. This is the 'rehabilitation' line, with twelve to fourteen colleagues down for one, two or three of each of our twenty-five lessons in the week. Thus the scheme costs twenty-five teacher-hours, the equivalent of one and a quarter full-time staff. Since this commitment does not infringe their normal allocation of free periods it depends on a slightly improved pupil-teacher ratio, which our founding authority, Northumberland LEA, was helpful in providing. The name of the scheme is drawn from the medical concept of improvement through therapy; the scheme's underlying precept is that all pupils however difficult are capable of adjusting their behaviour towards the values acceptable within the school society. As the year progresses pupils who exhibit acute behavioural problems can be withdrawn from their normal classes for a period of time and receive individual treatment in a one-to-one or small group situation.

A number of underlying fundamental principles have been established.

1   Rehabilitation is not a punishment. Disruptive behaviour rarely stems from original sin; it is usually a manifestation of a problem in the pupil's background, personality or stage of development, and it is the identification of this problem calmly and apart which is one of the two main aims of the scheme.
2   The needs of the majority come first. A school owes the strongest possible duty to its pupils to ensure that their lessons are carried on purposefully and in a disciplined way without hindrance from the few who are temporarily unable or unwilling to cooperate in the normal business of learning. By withdrawing the disrupter one permits teacher and pupils to proceed with their work without unreasonable tension.
3   Withdrawal is not a permanent measure. Rehabilitation implies restoring a pupil to regular classes once the problem affecting his or her behaviour has been identified and ameliorated. Usually pupils are withdrawn for either a week or a fortnight.

4   The scheme must be flexible. In many cases pupils who are disruptive in some classes are perfectly amenable in others, and when this is the case we use partial rehabilitation: the pupil remains in the groups and with the teachers where he or she has a useful working relationship and comes out of the others. Before withdrawing a pupil we always circularize the staff who teach him or her indicating that rehabilitation is envisaged and asking for comments. It is interesting that there has never yet been a universal thumbs-down: usually two or three staff report that the pupil is working satisfactorily and can remain within the group. Indeed comments are often quite explicit: 'Don't take him out of my class. He's doing well and I get on with him.' Nor is there a particular type of teacher from whom such comments come: one of the odd features about disruptive pupils is that they attach lifelines to unexpected people. That is one reason why a school needs alternatives to its normal pastoral system: some pupils react against the best head of house, year head or tutor.

5   It is not a way of avoiding work. If pupils are to be easily reabsorbed into their original classes they must continue to keep abreast of their work. We therefore have a teacher-coordinator whose function is to ensure that a sufficient supply of work reaches the pupil and his rehabilitation teachers. This is obviously easier in subjects that are not predominantly practical, and we have to accept the limitation that a pupil withdrawn from cookery, science etc will not be able to cover sections of the work.

6   Rehabilitation implies counselling. If we had a school counsellor as such the scheme would no doubt be of vital interest to him. However, in the course of a week the pupil will undoubtedly encounter one or more of our experienced heads of house as well as other sympathetic adults and is likely to talk freely with some of them. This low-key counselling is often natural and effective.

7   It is emphatically not an 'instant jankers' system. However attractive it might seem to a hard-pressed teacher to be able to instruct a recalcitrant to 'go and get rehabilitated', unilateral action would lose the qualities of calm and control which are essential. Before a pupil is withdrawn he will have shown some history of recurrent problems, in the course of which parents and staff will have been consulted and the system carefully explained to them.

8   It is not a 'unit'. Units are fashionable in education these days and no doubt valuable for some functions, but the word implies two conditions foreign to our scheme: special provision in terms of building and equipment and an identified place where it happens. Nothing would operate more certainly against the spirit of our scheme than a particular location defined as a 'sin bin'. The scheme must be an unobtrusive operation and must not have any associations with a place of confinement. All our pupils move about the building from lesson to lesson and most of them are on individual timetables (only the intake

year follows a common curriculum) so that pupils on rehabilitation moving from one teacher's base to another in no way stand out from their fellows. Given sensible communication, the receiving teacher knows whom to expect and can plan accordingly. I am very dubious indeed about the special units outside normal schools which some authorities are setting up to cater for difficult children: it seems in every way better for resources to be made available to schools that need them so that problems can be tackled within an environment where the majority of pupils are working normally.

9   It must not become a sink group. We decided at an early stage that the maximum number that the scheme could cope with at any one time was six.

Inevitably the scheme has been modified since its introduction. Initially it seemed right for me as head teacher to make the ultimate decisions about placing pupils on and taking them off rehabilitation, but it soon became evident that this was an unnecessary extra stage in the process. For several years now heads of house have made these decisions – they know the pupils very well indeed and inevitably take a major part in the sequence of contacts with pupils and their parents as problems emerge, recur and intensify; they are in the best position to weigh up and check in detail on the feedback from classroom teachers about disruptive behaviour and can judge when it is sensible to resist the demands of an individual teacher for the withdrawal of a particular pupil. In this way, rehabilitation properly becomes available to them as one of a range of techniques they can employ to cope with disruption and related problems – part of a pattern.

Initially it was intended that the scheme should be staffed by those colleagues who were positively interested in participating and that two hours a week were a sufficient stint for anybody. In the process of timetabling, however, it became clear that some staff who wanted to assist were more urgently needed elsewhere and that the scheme was the poorer for their absence. We have found that fourteen or so staff are too many for effective communication, and – even more important – some of them have expressed doubts about the effectiveness of their contact with seriously disturbed pupils when it was restricted to a couple of hours a week. The other main difficulty has been in maintaining a suitable flow of work from subject teachers and making it easily available to rehabilitation staff. At first responsibility was put on rehabilitation staff to ask subject teachers for work, and when this broke down because our scattered premises reduced the natural contact of one teacher with another a coordinator was appointed. Although this has improved the work flow, she has found the job unduly time-consuming, and subject staff at a remove from pupils on rehabilitation are understandably less interested in a problem that has at least temporarily gone away.

We are therefore now reorganizing the scheme so that it is directly operated by the six heads of house plus the coordinator; their average investment of time in the scheme is three or four hours a week, and this can be timetabled in complete half-days. In subject expertise these seven cover wide areas of the curriculum and are, in addition, our most experienced counsellors. They are all familiar with, and have ready access to, materials for the work in their subjects at the stages the pupils concerned have reached. When the coordinator can see that an important area of work is not covered by the natural subject interests of the new team, she asks subject teachers to supply material, but this is now a much less arduous chore. We have considered generating special materials and assignments for pupils on rehabilitation, but it is virtually impossible to cater adequately for a great range of subjects over three year groups without losing much of the flexibility and mobility of the scheme.

Does it work? Well, it has proved to be a useful aid to staff morale. We probably all remember that as young teachers undue demands were made on our personal resources by a few awkward pupils, and it is reassuring for young teachers to know that they are not bound to encounter these difficulties indefinitely and unaided. The very fact that a scheme of withdrawal exists has encouraged colleagues to persist in coping with problems longer and more constructively than they might otherwise have done. Teachers may well feel reluctant to send refractory pupils to head or deputies to be dealt with because of the implied reflection on their professional competence (others with less tender consciences may send them all the time, or – most futile of expedients – send pupils out of the room to kick their heels in the corridor). Rehabilitation is built into the system as a standard technique employed by the school, and staff use it as such.

Does it lead to an increase in truancy? Pupils absent themselves for a variety of reasons – because there is a problem looming at school which they cannot face, because they have alternative pursuits outside school which seem more attractive, because what the school offers seems to them irrelevant (of which more later), because they are useful at home and their parents connive in keeping them off, and for many more reasons. But school also provides most teenagers with their natural society and meeting-place, and the disruptive pupil in particular is very often an extrovert dependent on an audience. The truant is really a different issue, and we have not found that pupils stay away rather than go to rehabilitation classes.

Like all techniques it has a limited value and was by no means set up to be a cure for all ills. In particular, recurrent use of rehabilitation tends to be self-defeating, and we are reluctant to continue to use it several times over for the same pupil. In general, however, the scheme relieves pressure-points, gives time for consideration of individual cases, supports the classroom teacher and facilitates disciplined learning. Obviously it is dependent upon, just as it contributes to, the whole philosophy and practice of the school – in particular four main areas in which we see a direct link between what the school believes and does and the behaviour and attitudes of its pupils: administration; curriculum; sanctions; ethos.

Administration

All schools develop, according to size and complexity, the classic dual pyramids of power and administration – the academic and the pastoral, traditionally the academic has been preeminent. Many schools now have faculty systems which are more coherent than the rather scattered single-subject responsibilities which they have subsumed. For the purposes with which this article is chiefly concerned the value of the faculty unit lies in the fact that the performance of the staff as a whole has a significant effect on the total discipline of the school. A teacher encountering severe problems which he is failing to solve is a liability to his colleagues; the faculty system sets up enclaves of staff with related subject interests working ideally in close proximity and often combining in team teaching. Within this close society a new member of staff (or a student on teaching practice) can be absorbed, advised, backed up, given access to existing lesson material, engaged in groups researching new material. The process can be one of constant in-service training and is very supportive. Much potential disruption can be avoided if a group of teachers acts together to ensure that their lessons are well-planned, complementary and continuously brought up to date and if they act as a team when behavioural problems arise. It bears saying that all young teachers – and many more experienced ones – have discipline problems from time to time: there is nothing shaming about this, just as there is nothing shaming if a doctor has some patients whose symptoms do not respond at once to his diagnosis and medication. School organization can be positively designed to reduce the incidence and seriousness of behavioural problems. The traditional view of the isolated teacher – my classroom my quarter-deck, shut the door and keep out – cuts him off from one of his most valuable resources – the aid and experience of his colleagues.

The other facet of the power structure – the pastoral – is more obviously concerned with personal problems of all sorts. As pastoral structures develop in larger schools two main pitfalls seem to develop: a conflict between 'pastoral' and 'academic' interests and failure to grant sufficient status to those who run the pastoral side. This latter danger is of some real importance since a head of house or year frequently needs to negotiate with senior academic staff on an equal footing. (In passing, this crude distinction between 'pastoral' and 'academic' ought not to obscure the fact that all teachers have a dual role: indeed the teacher in the classroom, who may think of himself as primarily concerned with academic work, is in the very best position of all to identify early behavioural and other signs which indicate that a problem is developing. It is inescapable that all teachers are to an extent social workers and their initial training ought perhaps to take more notice of this.) In a large school with a substantial element of difficult children nothing contributes more to effective teaching than a well-developed pastoral system whose work, often unobtrusive, permeates the whole life of the school. There seems no good reason to suppose that there is anything inherently superior in either a house or a year system, or in a combination of the two: schools adopt a system usually because of the nature of the buildings they occupy, the age range they cater for and other constraints rather than because of deeply-thought-out philosophical preferences.

In our case a year system would have made little sense of three year groups and two main buildings, whereas our six houses conveniently divide three and three between the east and west wings. The system is devised primarily to ensure small enough units within a large school for every pupil to be well known, to have a geographical base in the house area and to know well at least two members of staff – the head of house and the form tutor. Our houses consist of two registration groups in each of years three, four and five – about 160 to 170 pupils – and a sixth-form tutor group which, though separate in many ways, retains a house allegiance. Heads of house teach half timetables (an investment equivalent to three full-time teachers) and have their own offices to which parents come directly just as heads of house visit them at home. This by-passing of senior management is fundamentally necessary because of the volume of parental visits and underlines the real power of heads of house. Together with his team of six tutors, the head of house is responsible for knowing pupils and their families in the same way that the head of a small school knows his and has charge of one-sixth of the buildings – fabric, tidiness, staff duty rosters etc. He has an overview of each pupil's academic progress, behaviour, social and sporting contribution to the school, personal happiness, career intention and prospects. Many problems are spotted at an early stage, others are dealt with promptly when they come to light, and the basic day-to-day matters of standards of work, behaviour and appearance are carefully checked.

Weekly meetings of the two policy-forming committees (heads of house with senior management and faculty heads with senior management) ensure that regular consultation and discussion occur. This too is costly – the equivalent of a full-time teacher – but it creates two clear lines of communication throughout the entire staff, because all colleagues are members of a house and of a faculty. A monthly timetabled joint meeting of heads of house, faculty heads and senior management promotes understanding of the specific problems of the academic and pastoral sides.

The curriculum
We are deeply convinced of the educational and social value of mixed-ability teaching; this conviction impinges directly on the question of disruptive behaviour. Wherever pupils are divided into separate groups by criteria of ability and/or attainment certain effects ensue. There is a correlation between low ability and anti-social behaviour: it is not an absolute correlation by any means, but where division by ability is practised the pernicious phenomenon of the sink group emerges, and the

sink group can be a disruptive influence not only within its own classroom but throughout the school. Such groups can take up disproportionate amounts of staff time and energy in what amounts to a containing exercise. Pupils simply being contained are not being educated, and that is a negation of what the school stands for. The classic sink group occurs in a rigorously streamed or setted organization. Banding undoubtedly alleviates this. However, even broad banding entails what are, for us, unacceptable implications. Pupils do tend to perform according to the teacher's expectation of their performance; they are not static units with a fixed intelligence marking a boundary through which they will never break. We still know little about the precise effects that the complex changes and pressures of adolescence have on a child's learning propensities. Yet we say to them at nine or eleven or thirteen 'you are in the fourth maths set' or 'you are in 1E' or 'you are in the CSE class', and thus we fix upon them the mark of our assessment of their limitations. Then we logically proceed to teach more advanced work to the first maths set, a second foreign language to 1A, and an entirely separate syllabus to the GCE class – thus ensuring that within a few months of the start of the academic year we have erected an obstacle course in the path of any pupil who develops rapidly enough to disprove our initial evaluation. Protagonists of streaming and banding claim that the horizontal lines they draw across their curriculum diagrams to indicate what is on offer to different bands or streams are really dotted lines rather than firm ones and that it is perfectly possible for pupils to be promoted(!) to more prestigious groups. I have never found that this applies to more than a handful of pupils, whereas I claim that the profiles of performance of individual pupils at thirteen and at sixteen in a mixed-ability organization with subject choice and individual timetables higher up the school differ quite remarkably in a substantial proportion of cases.

The application of these principles to behaviour is quite clear. We are often told that school curricula are 'irrelevant' to the problem-causing pupils. There is a great deal of confused thought about relevance in the curriculum: the school can provide little (nor would it wish to) that is' directly and vocationally relevant to, for instance, the boy who is going to work in a local factory and a girl who is going to serve in the supermarket. They will learn the restricted skills required 'on the job'. A school's main objective is broad education about the nature of man and his environment, and its aim must be to make such education available to all its pupils – available by putting on offer to all pupils all the learning resources of the school. Our experience is that this process is facilitated by that form of mixed-ability teaching which emphasizes individual guided learning rather than by the traditional class lesson.

It is often argued by opponents of this position that pupils are well aware of their own limitations and that there is something almost dishonest in offering them greater opportunities than they are manifestly able to cope with. I would reply by arguing that an intelligent adult often finds it

78

difficult to arrive at an objective assessment of his own skill compared with his fellows'; and adolescents are even less equipped for such self-analysis. Many undervalue themselves, have latent skills that they do not develop and sign off from intellectually demanding pursuits long before they have achieved their full potential.

Sanctions

All schools necessarily concern themselves with discipline, since without it there can be no effective teaching or learning, but we do not believe that traditional sanctions – beating, idiot essays and nonsensical 'lines' – have any relevance to the problems of adolescence in our time. If by 'the discipline of the school' we mean the sum of the behaviour of its pupils in and out of lessons, then it is clear that this is much more than a matter of rules and retributive sanctions to reinforce them: a flexible curriculum, a relaxed social ethos, the quality of formal and informal contact between staff and pupils are more far-reaching influences on behaviour than the narrow concept of 'punishment'. But there remains in every school a hard core of unacceptable behaviour: how is this to be dealt with? It won't be eliminated at a stroke! To defendants of the 'deterrent' theory I would point out that the punishment books of all schools I have been in that practised corporal assault indicated that the same pupils were punished again and again. The only effective solution is to alter behaviour patterns, and these will only change if attitudes are altered. This implies two things: systematic explanation to pupils of the reasons underlying civilized behaviour; facing them with the consequences of their acts, and demanding a defence of them.

The way children behave in school is in part also the responsibility of their parents, and parental support is an inestimable ally. We find that short suspension pending discussion between parents and school is a highly successful move in most cases, though longer suspension is highly suspect because a youth with time on his hands and nowhere to go is likely to find further trouble.

Extremely disturbed adolescents clearly need the help of external agencies, as do those with confirmed criminal tendencies. There is much that the school can do to help even these pupils, but the factor that makes the school situation unique and fraught is that while external agencies work relatively slowly the school often has to deal instantly with a severe problem. There is room for considerable improvement in the cooperation between external services and the school.

Finally

All living organisms – and institutions – evolve continuously, and the present time is one of remarkable activity in educational theory and practice. Looking back five years, it is clear that many of our techniques at Longbenton have changed quite radically, and this year we are undertaking a complete review of our fourth/fifth-year option system and its timetabling. But while changes in implementation of the school's philosophy are regularly effected, the bedrock beliefs with which we set out at the point of reorganization have been confirmed and deepened.

The curriculum makes accessible to all pupils all that the school has on offer in terms of subject options, staff expertise and resources of all kinds; and this implies that it is usually undesirable to organize teaching groups on the basis of the classified abilities of pupils.

In a civilized school community the traditional sanctions are irrelevant, while real discipline is more important than ever; behavioural problems are symptoms of pressure and distress rather than manifestations of original sin; we work to change attitudes, through attitudes behaviour.

While public examinations retain the importance they now have and significantly affect life-chances, all pupils are entitled to pursue courses which allow for their progressive development without cut-off points and which lead to a proper certification of their attainment when they leave school and of their effort and progress over the period preceding this point.

8 The curriculum and the disruptive child[1]

RAY JACKSON
Professor of Education, University of Malawi

When is a child being disruptive? Only teachers and parents are able to enlighten us here since they bear the brunt of such problems. Generally speaking pupils who are disruptive are those who interfere with the learning process by personally upsetting the teacher or members of the class or by encouraging other pupils to do so. The disruptive child may be backward or normal academically although the inevitable outcome of his negative behaviour is such that he often becomes a low- or under-achiever.

What are the *statistics* of the situation? One report suggests that 4 per cent of all London children are delinquents (TES 1974), while others indicate that between 4 and 10 per cent of all schoolchildren exhibit behaviour problems (Wall 1973). Individually such children have been variously identified as physically muscular, aggressive by temperament, generally hostile towards authority, less methodical than other pupils, tending to focus on the concrete rather than the abstract and as coming from less caring or less organized families (Lovell 1967). Yet another source suggests that eight of the most salient of forty-one major characteristics of American pupils who were a disturbance in class were, in order of importance, low socio-economic status, low-income family, work-rather than school-orientated, low mental ability, lacking in interest in school, retarded at school, parents anti or indifferent to school, and a long record of failure in school work, especially in reading (Blough 1965).

These pupils, like other individuals, have hopes, interests and expectations which must be respected. Maslow, for example, states that individuals have a hierarchy of needs which stem from bodily and security needs through the need for achievement, respect, love and ultimately for self-realization (Maslow 1957). But the curriculum in many secondary schools fails to provide the potentially disruptive pupil with what he requires in the way of adequate aims, security, organization, content and guidance facilities.

Any solution must depend upon the qualities of the staff and the number of disruptive and unresponsive pupils, but a number of suggestions are offered which may be adapted to particular circumstances.

The curriculum model offered in this chapter seeks to meet the needs of disruptive pupils more adequately than existing approaches and yet to be acceptable to teachers and society at large. A number of strategies are recommended:

1. the curriculum should consist initially of learning a basic core of traditional skills supplemented with free-choice open-ended topics;
2. a reappraisal of the aims of the school curriculum;
3. the compartmentalization of the school into smaller self-contained units;
4. at the middle and upper school levels the curriculum should be geared to public examinations;
5. at the lower school level the class teacher rather than the specialized subject teacher should predominate;
6. individualized learning should be encouraged where possible;
7. assessment should be biased towards the encouragment of expressive rather than cognitive attributes and towards the measurement of individual progress rather than comparison with group norms;
8. highly disruptive pupils should be allocated to a special class and expulsion might be considered for a few of the more serious cases;
9. a guidance system should be used to improve the efficiency of the curriculum process and to help with individual learning, emotional and subject-choice problems of pupils;
10. the prevailing theme should be cooperation rather than competition, senior teachers assisting new and junior teachers, more able pupils helping the slower ones.

Educational aims

One of the first problems of the school is to determine adequate educational aims. The success of many primary schools has in the recent past been measured by the number of pupils who 'passed' for the grammar school; the successful grammar school was one whose pupils had between them gained GCE O or A level passes, while direct grant school successes were measured by the number of Oxbridge scholarships taken by pupils. The school's objectives were in reality cognitive and curricular rather than expressive and personal. Dr Arnold, headmaster of Rugby, outlined the following aims in a sermon delivered in 1835 (Lauwerys 1965):

> What we must look for in this school is first – first in order of importance not merely first – religious and moral principle; secondly, gentlemanly conduct; thirdly, intellectual ability.

In other words, he believed that aims should be paramount and that cognitive aims were of secondary importance. This emphasis on expressive aims might well be reinstated with profit in today's schools.

The potentially difficult pupil often becomes actively disruptive in the classroom because high achievement levels in the various subjects are insisted upon. Douglas, in his monumental study of a group of individuals passing through the educational system, found that the achievement gap between A and C streams widened as they made their way through the school (Douglas 1964). Hargreaves, in a northern secondary modern school, embellished this by identifying an 'academic' sub-culture and a 'near-delinquent' sub-culture that became increasingly apparent as the pupil progressed through the school (Hargreaves 1967). Lacey, in a grammar school, found that those who were unable to cope with the academic work developed an 'anti-school' culture (Lacey 1970).

What *type of curriculum*, then, should be offered in schools? If academic studies are anathema to disruptive or potentially disruptive children, are progressive approaches any more acceptable to them? There is no clear evidence that they are. In schools pupils react in ways which indicate that they feel a lack of rigour in the courses designed for them, that they resent that, unlike more academic pupils, they are not doing a 'proper course'. Furthermore, the academic pupils will claim most of the 'prizes' in terms of examination passes. Lowenstein categorically allocates blame for violence in schools on progressive methods (Lowenstein 1974). Yet other more considered opinions suggest that certain pupils, especially those from the lower socio-economic groups, develop much more surely in highly structured classroom situations (Clegg 1974). Are we then to jettison the exciting and interesting new approaches developed by competent teachers and resort to the dreary academic grind? Is this an either/or situation? May we not develop a judicious blending of the two approaches so that as well as an element of variety there is an opportunity for the pupil to work in a structured situation for part of the day while other periods are devoted to freer and more open learning situations?

The school organization
Many disruptive pupils demonstrate personal characteristics of aggressiveness, lack of method and application in their working habits, and they tend to come from less well-organized homes. It is essential that they are allowed to work in a secure and structured environment at school. This means that attention should be paid to the organization of the school.

The organizational and work units in the school system are the whole school, the class and the individual, and when the school is large, say more than a thousand pupils, some intermediate organizational structure between the school and the class is often thought desirable, because the headmaster often loses 'touch' not only with the pupils but with his staff. Different types of organization can be adopted, for example, the house system, the year system and the system of lower, middle and upper schools. If the school has a preponderance of disruptive pupils, then some division of the school into small educational sectors may not only be advisable but necessary. I favour the lower, middle and upper school system, each under its own head, assisted by a triumvirate responsible for academic, pastoral and disciplinary matters. This form of organization should help staff to identify, contain and remedy the more disruptive elements in the school more easily. Thus difficulties concerning one part of the 'schools' may be kept separate from other parts, which may even be housed in different parts of the campus or buildings; different parts may start, finish and take breaks at different times and be serviced by a staff working solely within that particular part of the school. In this way staff responsibility for a particular section of pupils and the latter's responsibility to the staff are more clearly defined. The linchpin of the system is the head, who is responsible for both his staff and pupils and who, in turn, will be advised on policy by his triumvirate.

In the *lower school*, with eleven-to fourteen-year old pupils, each class will be taken for at least half its timetable by one teacher. If the class is particularly disruptive then the proportion of time it spends with one teacher might need to be increased. What is lost in not utilizing the skills of specialized staff should be gained by giving the pupil time to develop a relationship with an adult. Specialization will increase in the middle and upper school. In the case of a new or 'weak' teacher, he may wish to work in tandem with, and be advised by, a more experienced member of staff who has volunteered for, and receives credit for, this duty.

Thus the responsibilities of teacher and pupil are sharpened further. Much of their work will be done by pupils in their own classrooms. They will be offered an area of the school which is their 'own' and a teacher who is clearly their 'own'. In this way some of the insecurity which seems to plague some disruptive pupils may be lessened. Little security or 'feeling of belonging' is engendered in any situation which resembles Waterloo Station – a point to pass through rather than a place in which one can live and develop. Many pupils who are self-disciplined in classrooms are not always so in corridors and on stairways, and it is the disruption of the corridor which spills into the classroom rather than the other way round. Each teacher may have to be responsible for seeing that his class moves in and out of the school building in a reasonably orderly fashion. The playground and the sports field are the places where the pupils may give vent to their feeling. If the times of starting and finishing sessions vary between different parts of school this gives a ready-made reason for pupils to exercise restraint in the corridors and on the stairs.

The curriculum of the lower school should be partly formal/traditional; the morning sessions might be taken up with such work. The afternoons would be devoted to 'centres of interest' activities based on resource centres. The formal curriculum should consist of mathematics, English, history or geography, art or crafts or music, science etc, which are all typical of today's schools. Pupils should work on their own, from work cards or from texts, each with a daily assignment calculated well in advance for the whole month or term which he would be expected to complete and on which he would be assessed. Having completed his daily stint, he might choose to work on the next day's assignment or on any other previously agreed topic, for example a 'centre of interest'. An energetic teacher would prepare alternative tasks in case pupils choices were not thought suitable. Occasional class lessons would be given in all subjects to introduce new topics, to summarize others or to provide the opportunity of working together as a class. These sessions might be followed by graded exercises or by class or 'buzz' groups (small group) discussion. During these periods poor readers and writers would be identified by standardized screening tests and intensive efforts made to improve the quality of their skills. Use might be made of special groups within or outside the class, peripatetic teachers, volunteers and helpful parents, the child guidance clinic and the psychological services. While intensive efforts should be made in this direction (illiteracy, for example, is thought to be one of the factors associated with the incidence of disruptive behaviour) task mastery and other educational differences might also be tackled using similar techniques. The afternoon 'centres of interest' consist of individual choices based on a programme for several weeks mapped by pupil and teacher. Here the teacher acts not as a teacher (as in the morning sessions) but as a consultant/adviser, which should help to reduce the potential conflict situation between the teacher and the pupil.

The following strategies might be adopted:

1 The global centre of interest could be determined by the teachers in the form of a series of short courses for citizens or townsmen, model-makers, sportsmen, astronomers, sailing enthusiasts, 'social workers', musicians etc.
2 The pupils could devise and plan their own individual courses with the help of the teacher.
3 The teacher could choose with the class a common topic of interest which all pupils would follow.

Although pupils need variety, topics should be studied for long enough to be both viable and acceptable. Also, because pupils need both guidance and structure the teacher ought to provide them with a series of topic cards with suggestions on how to deal with them.

The 'core' of this curriculum is thus biased towards the traditional, with a progressive supplement. Teachers could enlarge any one sector to suit the particular class. At all events certain basic and key concepts and processes should be taught in each of the subject areas. In this way the timetable is 'harmonized'. This concept is important if a pupil is transferred, at his own or the teacher's request, from one class to another. It might be interesting to allow pupils as an experiment to choose in which class they would prefer to be during the following year.

An alternative approach might be mooted at this point. Assume that, for one reason or another, the progressive element in the curriculum is not considered suitable for the pupils and that the intention is to offer a more or less traditional, subject-oriented timetable in which pupils may work at their own pace. This timetable might be devised on the basis of the categories of Hirst (1970) or Phenix (1964) or the Schools Council (1972).

Pupils could then be asked to suggest which subject they find useful/useless or interesting/boring (Schools Council 1968). Parents might also be canvassed. The times allocated for interesting/useful subjects might then be extended and those for useless/boring subjects reduced. Similarly pupils might be asked what new subjects or topics they think should be included in the timetable. If it is impossible to include any of these subjects because of lack of space or time then a school club might be formed for those interested.

The *middle school curriculum* from the age of fourteen to sixteen will tend to be subject- or examination-oriented. Examinations are a part of life in a secondary school and many teachers fail to appreciate how they may be used to advantage. Indeed, more than 80 per cent of the relevant age group enter for some public examination. Guidance should be given to help pupils to choose suitable subjects. These may lead to GCE O level or CSE examinations and, it is to be hoped, to teacher-designed courses and examinations available through CSE Mode III provisions. The strength of this element of the course is that it is geared to pupils' choices and reflects their interests. CSE Mode III examinations and syllabuses enable teachers to meet the specific needs of pupils more adequately. All pupils should be entered for at least three examination subjects (CSE and/or GCE), although work should be graded on a lesson basis and on daily, weekly and monthly assignments. Teacher, parents and pupils ought to be involved in the subject choices. Alongside the subject lessons a careers/urban/rural life course should be organized in which all pupils would participate. The centre of interest groups could be organized as extra-curricular clubs.

The *upper school programme* given in the sixth form would probably not be plagued by so many disruptive pupils as those in the lower and middle school since staying on is voluntary. Work would still, as in the middle school, be subject-orientated and pupil, teacher and parent would still share in subject choice. Examinations aimed at would be GCE A and O levels, CSE and the new CEE examination, which is designed for those pupils who leave school at seventeen. Pupils of this age would have individual timetables, be given considerable privileges and be allowed to do private study at home or in the school library.

The careers and citizenship course. This course, taking perhaps one half day per week, would be devoted to a carefully selected programme of visits to hospitals, local government, the police station, churches, technical colleges and colleges of education, factories, farms, shops and offices and would also make use of films, visiting speakers and discussion groups. Here the parents may be of real help and they should be encouraged to speak to classes, to lead small groups and so on (Baxter 1973). Pupils should keep a record of visits and speakers and write reports and prepare and design appropriate charts and diagrams illustrating what they have seen and learnt.

Assessment

Assessment is necessary for all activities. Where possible it will be

86

continuous assessment since work in class will then count towards the final mark. Both the traditional and the centre of interest courses should be graded as well as those courses leading to examinations; not only would each day's achievement be graded but a separate grade would be given for effort and behaviour and norms or targets established. In one school known to the author grades are given for assignments in terms of cognitive achievement levels and efforts made and general behaviour. Each pupil must gain four high grades for behaviour, measured on a five-point scale, for four of his school subjects or activities. These may or may not be accompanied by high grades for achievement. Pupils falling below the behaviour 'norm' are required to explain the reason to the head, while in serious cases parents are interviewed; later still the pupil might be suspended and still later expulsion may be threatened. The importance attached to these behaviour grades means that pupils ought to be enabled to meet the norms and that in so doing their achievement levels will also improve. Every effort should be made to encourage high standards of work. Some schools put on a changing display of all aspects of pupils' work. This acts as a constant reminder of standards from the first few days and throughout the lower school. Disruptive pupils cannot easily abandon today's pleasure for tomorrow's profit. Thus success must be organized for them, not in terms of annual or term-ending examinations, which are too widely spaced to influence this type of child, but rather on a weekly or daily basis. Assignments should therefore be short-lived, assessment should be quick and feedback immediate. Continuous assessment is preferable to intermittent examination.

The most disruptive pupils should be removed from the ordinary class to special classes. In Inner London schools they are sent to a 'sanctuary' where they carry on with their own work. This might be regarded as a soft option by some pupils: in fact the special class should be a fully working class under the control of a senior member of staff who is a disciplinarian and has a facility for getting work out of pupils. Only the very serious cases should be sent to him, transfer taking place after discussion with the headmaster, the teachers concerned and the parents. Transfer to this class should be the penultimate stage before possible expulsion. The individualized curriculum should be 'harmonized' with that of the class from which the pupil came. One of the primary objectives of the school should be to rid itself of the need for this class by cutting down the number of seriously disruptive pupils. Whereas disruptive pupils will generally be regarded as relatively normal it would be impossible to take this attitude to members of the special class.

Guidance and counselling

It is essential that some system of explanation, rationalization and analysis of the curriculum and examinations should be made available for all pupils. The guidance system should include three teams of teachers organized at the lower, middle and upper school levels. Class teachers would act as tutors and would be allocated special periods on the timetable. A trained counsellor might be employed in some schools to help to coordinate guidance throughout the school. He would also suggest new guidance practices for approval by the school guidance committee and provide special testing programmes for teachers, at the same time acting as a link between the teacher in the classroom and the child guidance and school psychological services. A counsellor can formalize and professionalize all the potential guidance services of the school and can also offer opportunities for harnessing the community's guidance resources to the service of the school curriculum. Guidance personnel would also help the pupil and his work through 'general maintenance' procedures, that is they would identify, diagnose, and help to remedy the learning difficulties of pupils. Similarly they would help them to choose centres of interest in the lower schools and subject options in the middle and upper school. Parents would also be involved and before choosing subjects pupils would be given opportunities to see course texts, assignments, equipment and the like. 'Candidates' might be given an opportunity to talk to pupils already on the course and perhaps those who have left school, who might offer some 'independent' evaluation of the course.

Similarly, help would be given to pupils through career education and guidance. More important still the guidance personnel would help the individual by discussing with him his development, personal, social and academic, by attempting to offer a rationale for the curriculum, past, present and future, and by explaining the system of evaluation, examination procedure and techniques.

Extracurricular activities

Many disruptive pupils are non-joiners. To encourage their involvement in lower school activities extra-curricular activities might be linked with centres of interest, to teacher, pupil or parent leisure interests or to professional skills – thus driving or typing lessons might be offered, or a course in television repairs. An extensive extra-curricular programme will make up for the lack of pupil choice in the general curriculum. All these activities should be supervised, though pupils might help to draw up a programme. The main activities would take place during the lunch break, which might be extended if the clubs are well patronised. The non-joiners might be attracted by, for example, a 'pop music' club which could hold discotheque sessions during most lunch breaks whilst hearing talks about pop stars, traditional jazz, folk music, instrument-playing, the care of stereo equipment and the like.

Pupil/teacher/parent interaction

This programme depends in the main on the personality and enthusiasm of the teaching staff. Most pupils, even difficult ones, will respond to an organization which is designed to help them – both personally and vocationally – and which develops and recognizes their strengths and individual characteristics. Teachers should abandon the 'grammar school pupil model', who likes school work, is willing to prepare and sit for traditional written necessary examinations and probably does well with either a traditional or a progressive curriculum. The disruptive pupil and the rather slow learner must be considered *normal*. This may have the effect of changing teacher-pupil relations, which will not be based on the *conflict* model but rather on a *cooperation* or *bargaining* model.

Waller in a classic on teaching describes the problem as follows (Waller 1960):

> The teacher-pupil relationship is a form of institutionalized dominance and subordination. Teacher and pupil confront each other in the school with an original conflict of desires, and however much that conflict may be reduced in amount, or however much it may be hidden, it still remains. The teacher represents the adult group, ever the enemy of the spontaneous life of groups of children. The teacher represents the formal curriculum, and his interest is in imposing that curriculum upon the children in the form of tasks; pupils are much more interested in life in their own world than in the desiccated bits of adult life which teachers have to offer. The teacher represents the established social order in the school, and his interest is in maintaining that order, whereas pupils have only a negative interest in that feudal superstructure. Teacher and pupil confront each other with attitudes from which the underlying hostility can never be altogether removed. Pupils are the material in which teachers are supposed to produce results. Pupils are human beings striving to realize themselves in their own spontaneous manner, striving to produce their own results in their own way. Each of these hostile parties stands in the way of the other; in so far as the aims of either are realized, it is at the sacrifice of the aims of the other.

The kind of curriculum recommended does not remove the conflict model completely since the teaching of basic skills and elements of skill mastery emphasized must inevitably make possible difficulties between teacher and pupil. That said, attempts must be made to move away from this conflict model and towards that of cooperation. This may be assisted by the guidance and counselling system which should provide 'feedback' to the curriculum system and by the considerable powers of choice which pupils are given at *all* stages of the secondary school curriculum; extra-curricular activity provides further choices, as does the 'careers and citizenship course' in the middle and upper school levels, and both provide the chance to reduce conflict. An interaction model based on cooperation will be further enhanced by attempts by the staff to encourage pupils to help each other. Thus the slower pupil is helped by the one who finishes first. This may be expected of all pupils, and even the slower ones may be encouraged to attend younger classes and help slower ones there. Each pupil has an opportunity to help others and in this way it is hoped his self-esteem will grow and benefit.

Summary

The objective of the type of curriculum recommended is to provide a highly structured situation in which work assignments, although organized on an annual basis, are allocated weekly and daily to individuals. Grades are allocated for achievement, effort and behaviour, though attention should be paid mainly to the expressive (effort and behaviour) rather than the achievement grades. Thus the traditional, expressive objective of the school is restored to its previous position. Superior expressive grades should bring improvement in achievement levels. The traditional core of cognitive skills, especially reading, is supplemented by centres or topics of interest which may be of short or long duration. In these more experimental or integrated work may be given, up to half the timetable being devoted to them. Throughout emphasis is on the acquisition of satisfactory grades and on comparison with one's own past achievements. Transition to middle school brings with it a choice of subjects geared to CSE or GCE O levels. The guidance system previously geared to improving educational attainment by diagnosing strengths and weaknesses now focuses on decision-making and pupils should, with the aid of parents and teachers, be able to arrive at satisfactory choices. Each pupil will be encouraged to enter for three or more CSE and/or GCE subjects. A similar process continues in the upper school where the target examinations are CSE, GCE O and A level and perhaps CEE examinations. At these levels a careers and citizenship course of visits, films, speakers, tests and exercises is mounted and may include courses in cooperation with local technical colleges.

Generally the model is the average, sometimes unruly, boy or girl, who will work in situations which are often highly structured and receive assignments of short duration which proceed by logical steps.

Underpinning the whole system is a belief in helping others in a non-competitive atmosphere. Assessments should be meaningful but designed to advance rather than retard the development of self-esteem. The involvement of parents, especially in the guidance support for the system, is critical to success.

References

BLOUGH, T. B. (1965) reported in C. H. Miller *Guidance Services* New York: Harper and Row

CLEGG, A. (1974) quoted in the *Financial Times* 29 October and J. Payne (1974) *Teaching Materials for Disadvantaged Children* London: HMSO

DOUGLAS, J. W. B. (1964) *The Home and the School* London: McGibbon and Kee

HARGREAVES, D. H. (1967) *Social Relations in a Secondary School* London: Routledge and Kegan Paul

HIRST,P. H. and PETERS, R. S. (1970) *The Logic of Education* London: Routledge and Kegan Paul

LACEY, C. (1970) *Hightown Grammar* Manchester: Manchester University Press

LOWENSTEIN, L. F. (1974) 'School violence blamed on progressive ideas' *Daily Telegraph* 26 October

LAUWERYS, J. A. (1965) in 'General education in a changing world' *Comparative Education Society in Europe* Berlin: CESE 10

LOVELL, K. (1967) *Educational Psychology* London: University of London Press

MASLOW, A. H. (1957) *Motivations and Personality* New York: Harper and Row

PHENIX,P. (1964) *Realms of Meaning* New York: McGraw Hill

SCHOOLS COUNCIL SURVEY (1968) *Young School Leavers* London: HMSO

SCHOOLS COUNCIL (1972) *16-19 Growth and Response* London: Evans/Methuen

WALL, W. D. (1973) The problem child in the school *London Educational Review* 2, 3–21

WALLER, W. (1960) *The Sociology of Teaching* New York: Wiley; B. Geer 'Teaching' in B. R. Cosin *et al* (1972) *School and Society* London: Routledge and Kegan Paul; H. S. Becker (1953) The teacher in the authority system of the public school *Journal of Educational Sociology* 27, 128–41

[1] The author wishes to acknowledge his indebtedness to a number of practising teachers, more especially Mr G. I. Hook, Headmaster of Wisewood School, Sheffield.

9 Disruptive children in a community home

B. J. FLAHERTY
Stamford House Regional Assessment Centre

During the past few years the press has reported with alarming frequency the rapid deterioration and change in the way that we live with one another. Our society seems to be tearing itself apart: terror and violence internationaly, the rampaging of football fans and the aggressive behaviour of some children in schools frequently make the headlines. Although I am here concerned only with the increase of violence in classrooms, I believe that this is a part of a much wider upsurge of aggression in general life. Violence in the classrooms of some of our comprehensive schools is becoming commonplace and the vicious reactions of many pupils appear quite pointless and unrelated to the apparent cause; this would suggest that such acts are, at least in part, dictated by forces outside schools. Some education authorities are attempting to curb this violence by introducing special therapeutic units for young rebels and toughs who disrupt classes and who cannot be contained in normal day schools. The scheme has however already come under criticism.

One teachers' union is alarmed and horrified at the shocking increase of attacks on its members during the past year, the average increase over the past three years being about 6000 per cent. These attacks come not only from pupils but also from parents and relatives. Special conferences to discuss the problem have been arranged, and it is considered so serious that individual teachers have been requested to keep a daily record of incidents of misbehaviour in class. Teachers are undoubtedly working in stressful and demanding conditions.

This chapter attempts to review and comment on the incidence and variety of the types of behaviour generally described as disruptive, that is, conduct by an individual or individuals which has an adverse effect upon the proper working of a group. The setting chosen for observation is the classroom situation within the education department of a local authority's Social Services Department regional assessment centre where small groups of eight to ten adolescent boys are held temporarily in a semi-secure situation while reports on their social, educational, psychological and possibly psychiatric needs are compiled. As well as being composed of unsettled, disturbed, emotionally damaged and delinquent boys, the groups are continually subject to changes in composition because of daily arrivals and departures. There are also frequent interruptions in class because boys are required for interviews, medical examinations and individual testing by psychologists. The estimated daily turnover averages $12\frac{1}{2}$ per cent – thus one boy in eight leaves each day whilst another takes his place. There is nothing regular about this movement and a few days when numbers are stable may be followed by almost half the class leaving, to return either fully or only in part.

Classroom behaviour can best be examined in the context of group functioning. Groups never exist in isolation and are continually subject to change; their composition, size, structure and integration are all factors which determine their degree of cohesion and stability. Groups cater for the individual and collective needs of their members and during the course of their existence patterns of behaviour and ideologies can arise which have a profound effect upon the interaction of members, determining what is acceptable and unacceptable in terms of behaviour. Stott (1958) reminds us that 'we must think of groups as dynamic entities and not as mere collections of people haphazardly thrown together.' Some groups exist to safeguard and promote certain definite principles and beliefs; their membership is selective and voluntary. In industry and commerce task-dominated groups exist which to a large extent are selective and voluntary; some kind of contribution has to be made in exchange for tangible or intangible rewards and the roles of individuals are quite clearly defined.

The groups with which we are concerned within the assessment centre are to some extent selective but are not voluntary and may be more properly described as captive groups. Membership of these groups, at least on a conscious level, was not sought by the individuals they contain, and the normal regulative mechanisms which apply in voluntary groups are absent. In a captive group, especially when the membership is changing quickly, the norms and values which anchor the group are never really secured. There is a permanent temporariness about such groups and the tools of manipulation and control can never be used as effectively as in other groups. However, those responsible for organizing group activities need to have adequate knowledge of the factors which may hinder or prevent proper group functioning and must be able to take the necessary action for adjustment.

The groups described here differ from those within normal schools in the severity of their problems. The principles of group interaction involved, however, and the skills required to maintain these and to ensure the successful functioning of the groups are the same. Furthermore, especially in the case of ROSLA children, there is an element of compulsion about membership of groups within ordinary schools. Thus an examination of the more extreme groups will assist in the management of disruptive behaviour in the more conventional and less totally antagonistic groups in schools.

In such an unstable and potentially disruptive situation, which presents a continual challenge to the teacher's skill, it is remarkable that there are few really serious incidents. Some difficulties are minimized by the teacher's general awareness, which he develops surprisingly quickly, and also by his knowledge of the individual case histories of his pupils. Unexpected problems demanding immediate solution can arise quickly and special services may be enlisted.

Disruptive behaviour may be conveniently categorized as overt or covert, deliberate or unintentional, and its causes may be far removed from their manifestation. Misbehaviour in school or home can originate in and become manifest in either place, so we have a complicated four-point variable. A lad may cause mild disruption without incurring the displeasure of the class. He is mischievous in a harmless and acceptable way without transgressing group standards and merely provides a humorous temporary diversion enjoyed by all. Similar behaviour from another member may immediately invite group hostility. An in-depth investigation of the root causes of an individual's disruptive conduct is impracticable in the classroom, but a knowledge of general causative factors is essential in coping with it. It is important that the class teacher should know how the particular child is regarded by other members of his group and how far the mild disruption that he is causing is essential to him. The teacher needs to be an opportunist, flexible in approach and able to use initiative in organizing individual and group activities, and to be prepared for variety and change at short notice. If he can cope successfully with these minor disruptive incidents he will satisfy two considerations: he will protect the client by exercising caring functions and he will preserve the operational climate of the group. One must not be sacrificed at the expense of the other, however.

The following are descriptions of a few disruptive situations which occur in the classrooms of the assessment centre.

Two boys may have a very adverse effect upon each other. Perhaps they have been confederates in law-breaking and are pursuing deviant activities with little regard to their consequences. The very presence of one triggers off in the other the type of conduct for which they share responsibility – pushing, pulling and chasing each other; each feels that their combined misbehaviour absolves them from individual blame. They quickly accuse each other, but it is all very much a fun situation. When events take a serious turn there is either a conspiracy of silence or each will defend the other, even finally admitting guilt when innocent in an attempt to discredit the system. Involvement in a crash activity programme which really appeals to their interest and which involves both in a profitable partnership, especially if the teacher is also fully participating, may at least temporarily solve the disruption. Obviously each achieves great satisfaction from his involvement with the other, whether it be for delinquency outside the assessment centre or for disruption within it; equally, if they are properly organized, they may be satisfied by working together on more positive activities.

Another situation that frequently arises in the classroom is that a lad has a genuine distaste for a subject; this may only be revealed by his disruptive conduct – playing around, accidentally breaking pencils, delaying tactics, irrelevant questions etc. In a practical lesson in which a boy is producing a permanent record of his limitations in the form of a piece of pottery, woodwork or metalwork, he may be disappointed and frustrated in not being able to achieve, and so he has to destroy. In desperation he often acquires the work of another pupil and may destroy it too. This causes friction and disruption, and the sympathetic teacher will deal with the matter privately. In the long term the pupil's progress can be carefully monitored, which will be meaningful to him, but in the immediate situation the problem can often only be overcome by the introduction of a novel measure, in the shape of simple and repetitive work which gives quick achievement to avoid frustration.

The overactive lad in class can be a source of real disruption. He is anxious and tense, unable to organize himself or his efforts even for short periods and interferes with the work of others. When he manages to ruin someone else's work, which he invariably does, the situation can become explosive, and no amount of apology seems to ease the crisis. Regardless of recriminations from fellow-pupils or censure from the teacher, this type of boy acts compulsively. He has no thought for the consequences and appears unaware that his behaviour results in so much disruption. In the short-term he must be given real responsibility, and this often seems to surprise him. Acting as the teacher's aide de camp often transforms his behaviour. This manoeuvre is usually fully accepted by other pupils, for children are perceptive in such cases and are prepared to make allowances for the poorly adjusted child. Under no circumstances must the teacher feel himself to be the victim of intimidation or bribing and he must reserve the right to reverse his decision at any time.

Temper tantrums, which can be very emotionally loaded and time-consuming for all concerned, require firm and positive initial action. The child is upset, angry and often loses control, and he must be quickly prevented from injuring himself or other people or damaging property. This can only be achieved by the teacher's intervention. If the child needs physical restraint then it is advisable to remove him from the class until an investigation can be made. Often hostility shown against the teacher and fellow-pupils is the climax of a series of frustrating incidents and relationships with other children, teachers, house-masters and social workers and the cumulative result of many difficulties. If at all possible the teacher must make the child feel that he is understood and that every effort will be made to deal with the problem as quickly as possible. Other pupils are often able to help in this reassurance. Some temper tantrums are feigned, however, as a cover or diversionary tactic, and in these cases the teacher must make the culprits aware that their techniques are transparent.

Teachers must also be conscious that enmity or jealousy can gradually be built up within a class group or be imported from outside school by a new member. If the rivals happen to be of different nationalities the situation can become dangerous, for well-meaning individuals are prepared to support their friends in sniping actions or occasional acts of open aggression. Mixed groups can very easily fragment themselves into a kind of gang warfare unless adjustments can be made, and therefore the teacher must continually look to the possibility of restructuring his group and dispersing some members to other classes. The ringleaders must be made conscious that the teacher is aware of what is going on, and in all cases they must be confronted with a positive attitude which leaves them in no doubt about the inadvisability of their attempts to incite aggression in their classmates.

Sometimes direct verbal abuse from a poorly adjusted child has to be dealt with in front of an audience. Temporary removal from the group until the child can return voluntarily on request may be the best course of action. Confrontation must always be avoided in such cases so that a professional learning and teaching atmosphere is preserved in the classroom. The teacher should not feel that he need immediately assert his authority in public, for often the child will quickly feel that he has acted wrongly or misbehaved badly and will wish to apologize. Such an apology should always be accepted quickly; it has the effect of cementing a loose relationship with the child, who will now feel that the teacher has a personal and sympathetic understanding of his problems.

Abscondence from class can have a very disruptive effect on those who remain, very much as truancy has in ordinary schools. The seriousness of being absent without leave is often not appreciated until it is explained. Normally it occurs before a boy is due to return to court or transfer to another home and in such cases is obviously the result of increased pressure upon the child. Quite often, however, boys abscond on the spur of the moment when the opportunity presents itself. It is likely that the teacher will feel responsible and guilty when one of his charges leaves him, especially if the absconder becomes involved in further offences. Some absentees return voluntarily within a few hours, others are escorted back by parents, police or social workers. Each case should be dealt with according to its seriousness, but always in the interests of the child. Younger pupils, homesick and worried about their parents, are usually returned to their groups after a counselling talk by a senior member of staff. Older boys who commit further offences while they are absent may disrupt a class on their return and must be firmly instructed not to discuss any of their escapades with their fellow-pupils. Experienced members of staff can usually read the signs when a boy intends to abscond and can counsel the boy or cater for his interests.

Among a group of unsettled children disruption can happen at any time. Trivial incidents are suddenly magnified and can trigger off more serious incidents. School caretakers are fully aware of the 'forgetful' pupil who lets the water flood the washrooms and pushes Plasticine into keyholes;

teachers are aware of pupils who damage and waste materials, who paint themselves and friends in the art room or who borrow property without permission and forget to return it. All these incidents are disruptive and hinder the smooth routine of a class or school, but to detect them is very difficult and impossible within set time limits. Stealing, cheating and lying can be most disruptive forms of behaviour and possibly form part of a pathological pattern.

Dealing with emotionally disturbed and unsettled children, especially in a learning situation, makes many demands on the teacher but brings him many compensations. The temporary nature of an assessment centre, with mixed age groups, a wide ability range and different cultural problems all combined in a moving population, makes considerable demands, and the teacher must continually reappraise the group with which he is involved.

Some of the foregoing may be regarded as minor forms of disruptive behaviour which can be successfully coped with in the smaller classroom groups. The more difficult classroom problems require immediate and decisive action, but the teacher must always guard against any form of personal emotional involvement, because some forms of misbehaviour can be extremely distasteful. Types of misconduct that most teachers find unacceptable include violence towards other pupils or staff, threatening behaviour, deliberate damage to property, insolence, obscene language and vulgarity or any open challenge to or defiance of reasonable requests. The individuals involved usually have some history of rebellion towards society or school or, if beyond school age, they probably have a poor work record and are very anti-authority. With such damaged and unsettled individuals a trivial incident often gets out of porportion. A lad may fail to integrate properly in the group and may feel himself rejected and ridiculed because of his inability to measure up to group performances and achievements. More often than not his rebellion will have a personal source: he may be bewildered and angry because his parents have not visited him or because he has not had any mail. He feels very much an outcast and is prepared to rebel at the slightest imagined provocation. His negative experiences warp an already damaged personality and his reactions are already assuming a pathological form. It must be remembered that young people who disrupt the normal routine of school do so because of an accumulation of personal problems in conjunction with suddenly intolerable group pressures.

During the past few years many court judgments have increasingly stressed the caring function of teachers, particularly when they are exercising responsibility for the physical, intellectual and social needs of clients whom the law has placed in care in a special residential establishment. The dilemma is that the action taken must be in the interest of the client as well as for the benefit of the group as a unit. Removal from the group for whatever reason can be extremely damaging and is nothing but an emotional amputation. In such circumstances the teacher must rely on his own personal resources rather than on textbook instructions. Even an older adolescent may be alarmed and distraught when he loses control and may also become tearful and repentant. Others in the group may then become ruthless in condemning and transferring their own guilt, but they can also be surprisingly sympathetic and understanding when witnessing real distress. Occasionally the wise and experienced teacher can judiciously turn a blind eye, thereby gaining moral support from the group, which recognizes the difference between the teacher's real strength and the weakness of the child.

Persistent indiscipline and aggressive behaviour necessitate temporary or permanent transfer to another class, but haphazard change only exacerbates the problem. When a transfer is really necessary it must quickly be established that the receiving group is suitable and ready to absorb and cater for an unsettled new member. While an individual teacher is responsible for maintaining the discipline of his class, the head of department, the teacher concerned and the client are all involved in making a successful transfer. In another group with a new teacher, new fellow-pupils (possibly of a slightly different age range) and new activities and timetable, a remarkable and almost instantaneous change in behaviour often takes place. Children often bury their differences while adults hold a *post mortem*. But it must be stressed that change for change's sake will not automatically benefit either the child or the class. Such changes must be carefully planned and the receiving group must be examined to ensure that it will afford the disruptive child a more helpful environment.

In a boy's own interest and for the protection of other persons it may be necessary to place him in secure accommodation, and in these cases the most stringent rules apply. Confinement must not exceed forty-eight hours in seven days, either continuously or as two separate periods each of twenty-four hours. Further extensions may be approved by the local authority responsible for the centre, but in all cases the care authority, that is, the authority responsible for the boy, must be informed. The care authority has the right to remove a client from a secure accommodation but then becomes responsible for making alternative arrangements for him.

The extremely disruptive and uncontrolled boy who resorts to violence and forfeits his liberty is desperately in need of understanding and support regardless of the 'offence'. His temporary isolation must be regarded by those in charge as presenting an opportunity for advice and counselling, for a modification of attitudes and for involvement in a variety of closely supervised situations in an organized setting. The lad has time to review past events at leisure, to receive guidance at the time he requires it and to place things in perspective. The therapy is designed to help him to establish a better relationship with his fellows. His progress is carefully monitored and all relevant information presented in a special conference where members of several disciplines are represented under the head of assessment. Within the secure accommodation a client is 'specialled', that is, he is able to indulge in the luxury of a one to one relationship with a member of staff.

Despite his physical restriction he is able to receive and contribute towards intensely personal and individual casework in a secure but action-filled climate. Every effort is made to offset frustration due to loss of liberty. Depriving children of freedom invites much justifiable criticism and professional social workers are showing much concern. Until alternative methods of treatment can be developed, the positive aspects of detention must be clearly preserved.

In conclusion, it should be stressed that the children with whom this chapter has been concerned are essentially those who are encountered in normal classroom situations. These children have come from ordinary schools and after a period in the assessment centre some return to ordinary schools whilst others proceed to community homes. What has been said of the behaviour of these children in the more restricting and structured environment of the assessment centre is true of them in their normal classrooms. Similarly, therefore, their management in the classrooms of the assessment centre has relevance to their management in their original schools. Disruptive behaviour in class is a very variable quantity which depends upon many changing factors and is open to a wide variety of interpretations. The antecedents of the behaviour must be taken into consideration and what is known of the child and of his home environment must be kept constantly in mind. The teacher should ask whether it is likely that a particular incident is an isolated one or whether it belongs to a sequence which is likely to continue. The degree of involvement of others is also a particularly important consideration at this time. Above all in any incident of disruption the teacher must give priority to the needs of the disruptive child.

10 The role of the supportive services

JOHN STROUD
Assistant Director of Social Services, Hertfordshire

It will be clear from other chapters in this book that children who present problems in the school setting are far from forming an homogeneous group. This needs particular emphasis if it is accepted that such children cannot be seen in isolation from family, cultural and social influences. To take an example, an aggressive child may be reacting against a repressive, autocratic father, or he may have a weak father or no father at all; he may have abnormal brain-rhythms; he may have suffered emotional damage in early childhood; he may be under the influence of a neighbourhood gang; he may be protesting against a serious marital conflict between his parents; or he may be disadvantaged because of a combination of several of these factors.

This being the case it will be obvious that the social services, defining that term in its widest sense, will play different roles and intervene in different ways at various stages of a child's life. For example, the quality of care which a child receives during the formative years from birth to five, before he even enters the school system, will significantly affect his performance and behaviour in school when he is in his teens. To some extent therefore a description of the health visitor service, or of the playgroup movement, or of the adoption process, is by no means irrelevant, for the better these services the smaller the incidence of profound disturbances in the schools.

Here, however, we come up against the problem of space, because in a short chapter such as this there has to be stringent selection from the mass of information available. The law relating to the care and treatment of children 'in trouble' runs to over a thousand pages in the standard textbook; the range of duties undertaken by a local authority Social Services Department is so great that a whole book could be devoted to them alone, and indeed whole books have been written on such narrow sectors as adoption or foster-home care.

Further, although it may be accepted that social attitudes and values and political policies may affect the *volume* of delinquency and disruptive behaviour, the reasons why an individual child becomes delinquent or disruptive are likely to be unique to that child and his family and their patterns of relationship, and are also likely to be complex. This is, in short, an area where generalizations are more than usually dangerous, and given the exigencies of space there is a real risk of over-simplification. The notes which follow must be read with that in mind and should be regarded as signposts, not as formulated remedies.

My plan has been to indicate something of the contribution which each of the agencies can make to the solution of a problem and the powers which they may exercise and to focus in particular on methods of work with children of secondary school age. Once again a *caveat*: though a power may exist, the way in which it is exercised may vary and will certainly not be rigid and predictable. For example, Social Services Departments have two statutory responsibilities which are almost contradictory: to bring children before the court 'as in need of care and control' and, under another Act, to *diminish* the need to bring children before a court. It will be for a social worker to decide, on the best information he can collect from his colleagues, whether court action or casework with the family is likely to achieve the best result in the shortest time. The decision will rest on a careful diagnosis of an individual case. Similarly the police have wider powers to exercise discretion than is generally realized.

Social Services Departments are administered by the County Councils, Metropolitan District Councils and London Borough Councils (thus outside of the large conurbations the Director of Social Services is on the same level as the County Education Officer). They were formed in 1971 by an amalgamation of the old children's and welfare departments plus some services (e.g. for mental disorder and home helps) previously administered in health departments.

These departments carry out a very wide range of duties which may usefully be discussed in terms of primary, secondary and tertiary prevention, using a medical model. The departments are not merely 'preventive' agencies, however, and are concerned to promote good social health – if by that we may accept the notion of 'building a caring community'.

Primary prevention
Many departments employ community workers who are not concerned with the treatment of individual problems but try to help communities to grow and develop. Thus, for example, they might stimulate the formation of self-help groups. The departments provide facilities for certain groups of people who may be 'at risk' – thus day nurseries for unmarried or deserted mothers; it is not always realized that such establishments exert considerable influence on the standards of child care throughout the locality. Departments are also responsible for registering and supervising a number of private and voluntary projects ranging from pre-school playgroups to old people's homes and through these activities they strive to raise the standards of caring in the community.

Indeed, Social Services Departments have to an uncomfortable degree to identify and encourage generally accepted norms of behaviour, and this presents many moral conflicts, particularly in the field of working with adolescents.

Secondary prevention

The departments offer a wide range of services to individual families who are 'failing to cope' and are also in a position to mobilize help from other sources if necessary. In most cases the initial diagnosis of the problem, followed by recommendations of possible solutions, will be carried out by a social worker. Social workers are usually organized in teams covering a particular town or district, and each team may include specialists – in mental ill-health or in physical disability for example. The social workers will initially try to seek a solution, or at least some amelioration of the problem, *in situ*: that is to say, within the family or within the locality. Thus, for example, if a person has suffered a serious accident paralysing him from neck to feet, the social worker will try to help by adapting the home and providing special aids rather than by removing him to institutional care.

Similarly, in the field of child care the social worker will be anxious to try to preserve the child's home for him, bearing in mind the volume of evidence demonstrating the damaging effects upon the child of removal or separation. Thus, if the child is neglected because of parental malfunctioning, the social worker will try to tackle the malfunctioning rather than remove the child hastily.

This general philosophy has been frequently misunderstood, and social workers have been accused of failing to remove children quickly enough from a dangerous environment. Occasionally this is because of a legal problem. Social workers have no more power than the ordinary citizen: in order to remove a child they must obtain a legal order, and in order to obtain an order they must satisfy a magistrate that there are genuine grounds for concern. Usually however the social worker steers so to speak between Scylla and Charybdis. The dilemma is most acutely illustrated in the so-called 'battered baby' case. Babies do suffer profound emotional disorder from changes of care, and yet they may also suffer profound physical damage from an over-wrought parent. This dilemma is more subtle in the case of the neglected school-age child, who may have lived all his life in an unsatisfactory home and be unable to adjust satisfactorily to a substitute home.

The social worker, in short, is concerned to help a child to develop into a reasonably well-adjusted and competent adult; and in by far the majority of cases this is best done by helping the child without separating him from his family. But this approach, which tries to deal with a problem *in situ* and on a long-term basis, may lead to misunderstanding and conflict, for example in the field of non-attendance at school. The teacher, knowing that a child's schooling is of comparatively short duration and that a six-months' absence will be ruinous, sees the objective as the return of the child to school; but the social worker may see non-attendance as only a symptom of grossly impaired relationships at home and realize that unless these are put right the child's whole personality may be irretrievably damaged. In such cases close liaison and consultation should develop between teacher and social worker, but unfortunately it rarely does.

There is sometimes conflict of opinion over the desirability of taking a child to court for non-attendance, or indeed on some other ground of neglect or lack of parental responsibility. It should be noted that the Children and Young Persons Act 1969, the statute which governs such proceedings, not only requires the social worker (who usually takes the case to court) to prove that the child is neglected or 'not receiving efficient full-time education suitable to his age, ability and aptitude' but *also* to prove that he is unlikely to receive the care and control he needs without a court order. The implication of this is that the social worker has to go to *considerable* lengths to solve the problem without recourse to the courts.

Tertiary prevention

There are of course many cases – a sizable minority – in which the family situation is irremediable. Sometimes a family does not even exist: both parents may have deserted, or a single parent may have died. Sometimes the malfunctioning of the family is serious and intractable. In any of these situations the focus of attention must narrow to the individual who is 'at risk' and to the consideration of some form of substitute care, treatment or training. Such alternative care may range from the adoptive home for the baby whose mother cannot care for him to the compulsory admission to hospital of a mentally disordered adult. As far as disturbed, delinquent or neglected children are concerned, they may have to enter the care of the local authority. Such care may be arranged either on the voluntary application of the parents, in which case the Social Services Department has at present little power to control the timing or circumstances of the discharge of the child[1], or by means of a care order made by a juvenile court.

Most of the delinquent and wayward children are so 'committed' to care. (It should be noted that 'a child' in this context is a person who has not attained his seventeenth birthday.) A care order lasts until a child's eighteenth birthday (or, if he was sixteen when committed, until his nineteenth birthday), although both local authority and parents can apply at any earlier time for the revocation of the order.

A care order is not the only type of order that the magistrates can make. They can make a supervision order, choosing either a probation officer or a social worker as supervising officer; they can make an order committing a mentally disordered child to an appropriate hospital; if an offence has been committed they can fine a child or order him to a detention centre. If faced with a particularly refractory older child, however, they cannot themselves make a Borstal order: they must remit the case to a higher court for sentence.

When a care order has been made, it is entirely for the local authority

103

Social Services Department to make the appropriate placement – including the return of the child 'on trial' to his own home
when the time is ripe. Younger children may be placed in foster-homes or
community homes, or occasionally in boarding special schools; older ones
in lodgings, hostels or in community schools (still widely though
erroneously referred to under their old name 'approved schools'). The
Department may transfer a child, say from a home to a school, if this would
better meet his needs.

Concern has been expressed about this power of the Social Services
Department and about the operation of the 1969 Act. Much of it springs
not so much from the Act itself as from the chronic shortage of resources of
all kinds, in particular of residential staff willing to live and work with a
congregation of such disturbed youngsters.

New methods of working are constantly being explored, and mention
should here be made of the concept of 'intermediate treatment'.
Magistrates have the power to insert 'requirements' into a supervision
order, which require a youngster to reside away from home for a short
period (up to ninety days) for intensive treatment, or alternatively to
attend at some specific centre on a daily basis. The development of
effective measures is the responsibility of the Social Services Department.

The police

The police have a general duty to 'keep the Queen's Peace', to detect crime
and also to prevent it, and to prosecute offenders against the law. Their role
in detecting crime and prosecuting offenders is fairly well understood. It
should be remembered that between one third and one half of all *offences*
are committed by persons under the age of twenty-one, though many of
these offences are petty and irritating: they are difficult to detect and a
detection-rate of 50 per cent is creditable. A child who has not reached his
tenth birthday cannot be prosecuted under criminal law, even though he
may have committed an offence. He can however be brought before a
court as being 'in need of care and control'. Common police practice is to
'warn' such young children and to report the matter to the Social Services
Department for appropriate follow-up action.

Children of all ages below seventeen can of course be brought before the
courts as 'in need of care and control' and the police are fully empowered
to proceed in this way. They must however consult with the Social Services
Department before initiating action, and more and more often these days
they request the Department to take whatever action is appropriate.

When an offence has been committed by a child who has attained his
tenth birthday, the police may proceed by prosecution. They have,
however, considerable powers of discretion: they may for example decide
not to proceed if the child in question is obviously mentally disordered and
arrangements are in hand for his treatment. Increasingly the police are
making use of the official caution: practice varies slightly but in most forces

the children cautioned have not 'come to notice' previously and have admitted their guilt. Cautions are administered in almost half the cases of offences committed by juveniles and are clearly effective. In addition to official cautions, which are recorded, the police can of course make use of their traditional powers of informal warning.

As far as disruptive older children are concerned, the police will themselves take action in respect of a child only if he has committed an offence. An outburst by a group of youngsters will be dealt with as a breach of the peace, but only if it occurred in a public place.

The police do have powers to deal promptly with cases of children found severely ill-treated or neglected: unlike the social worker, who has to apply to a magistrate for what is called a place of safety order, a policeman can on his own authority remove a child to a place of safety (although within eight days he must produce the child before a juvenile court).

Education Welfare Officers

At the time of writing this service is under close and careful scrutiny, for although it is old-established and has honourable traditions it has drifted into something of a 'Cinderella' situation. The training, status, deployment, supervision and duties of EWOs vary enormously across the country, as the recent report of the Ralphs Committee clearly showed.

In its early days the service was primarily concerned with attendance at school, or rather with non-attendance; and a non-attendance problem is still normally referred first to the EWO for diagnosis and treatment. Over the years, however, the service has taken on other duties – for example, the administration of maintenance or necessitous clothing grants, the verification of applications for free school meals, and liaison duties in respect of special education.

Because of these miscellaneous duties, it may be said that EWOs often have the role of 'front-line trouble-spotters'. A problem of non-attendance, or sporadic attendance, is often a symptom of a deeper disturbance in the home while investigation of an application for free school meals may reveal a number of interlocking domestic problems. Unfortunately, however, the service, like so many of the caring professions, is undermanned, and many EWOs have to cover so large a geographical area, and so wide a range of duties, that they find it difficult to undertake therapeutic work with individual families. There is much confusion at present about the respective roles of the EWO and the social worker and clarification is urgently required.

One of the problems for the teacher confronted in the classroom with 'a child with problems' is whether to refer the case to the EWO, the psychologist, the social worker or the school doctor. It may be helpful to regard the EWO as the eyes and ears of the school in the domestic situation, as the first person to make an appraisal of the background and to mobilize such help as may be necessary.

Child guidance

This is the title originally adopted by the movement in the 1920s, but nowadays a variety of titles is appearing: perhaps 'child and family psychiatric service' gives the most accurate description of the approach adopted. The original concept was of a diagnostic and therapeutic team consisting of child psychiatrist/therapist; educational psychologist; and specialist social worker. Such a team might take on the assessment of children presenting learning difficulties or apparently in need of special education; the provision of reports on children appearing before the juvenile courts; the treatment of children with emotional hang-ups or of parents interacting badly with their offspring; and the provision of support and counsel to teachers, social workers and residential staff involved in difficult situations. The organization of the service, its quality and its selection of priorities, however, varies widely across the country.

This service, like so many others, is badly under pressure at the moment because of the high rate of demand and because of an acute and persistent shortage of staff, particularly of medically-trained personnel. Many clinics can only rely on a part-time or sessional consultant. Such therapeutic work as can be accepted is often undertaken by the social worker, whilst the educational psychologist in the team may take on the role of adviser and consultant to teachers, residential workers etc.

There is also a problem of a different kind – a psychological problem, of which there are still lingering traces. Most of us, though we might not admit it, are still somewhat in awe not only of mental illnesses but of those who specialize in them. We regard the latter to some extent as magicians and witch-doctors – popular reference to a psychiatrist as a 'head-shrinker' betrays how much primitive feeling remains in this area – and are only too pleased to transfer a baffling or frightening case to their care. Child guidance teams have in the past perhaps too often colluded in such transference so that cases are taken on without any feedback to the teacher and sometimes without any on-going involvement on his part.

Today, with disturbed children appearing in the classrooms in what seem to be greater numbers, it seems that this type of 'handing over' for treatment is unrealistic. What is unclear is the extent to which teachers can realistically make use of the diagnostic, advisory, supportive and therapeutic skills of the clinicians, and some hard thinking is necessary in this respect.

It should be borne in mind that the clinical teams possess few authoritative powers. They may be involved in ascertaining that children are in need of special education, though it is for the education authority itself to administer the directive power. Most, but not all, medical consultants are authorized to command compulsory hospital treatment for mentally ill or severely mentally handicapped children. The clinic social workers, now employed by Social Services Departments, have theoretically the power to initiate 'care and control' proceedings, though there are certain practical problems still to be overcome. In general terms it may be said that psychotherapy has the best chance of success when the child and his parents cooperate voluntarily and there is no element of compulsion. If this is the case, simply to 'send' a child into therapy may be foredoomed to failure.

Probation
Like so many of the social services, which are developing at different rates in the face of rapid changes in society itself, the probation service too is at present evolving, though quite slowly. Emphasis is shifting from the juvenile to the adult offender. Long-established teachers will recall that twenty years ago the local probation officer was often their first 'port of call' when they were concerned about a wayward child, and the PO would often offer to tackle the problem on an informal or voluntary basis. Some children in school would be 'on probation' and their supervising officer would be in close touch with teachers and become a familiar figure in the school.

This service is still offered, perhaps most noticeably in rural areas; but little by little, as they become better equipped, the Social Services Departments are taking over work with juveniles. Before the implementation of the 1969 Children and Young Persons Act, probation officers were involved with young offenders in three ways. First, when they were informed (usually by the police) that a child was to be brought before the court for an indictable offence, they would prepare a social enquiry report, which would contain information about the child and his family, including a school report and often a recommendation to the magistrates of the most appropriate treatment. This report would be presented to the court only after the child's guilt had been proved. Secondly, if the child were put on probation, the probation officer would supervise. Thirdly, and especially in the case of an older child, if he were sent to what was then called an approved school the PO would act as 'after-care agent' for a fixed term after the child's discharge from the school.

As we have already seen, this third requirement was completely swept away by the 1969 Act: children are now made subject to care orders and local authority social workers undertake post-training supervision. Social workers have now also taken on the task of preparing social enquiry reports in respect of all children under the age of fourteen. Probation orders have also disappeared in favour of supervision orders; whilst the Act states that a court may choose either a probation officer or a social worker as the supervising officer, in practice probation officers normally take on those aged fourteen and upwards. Meanwhile increasing concern about prison after-care, Borstal after-care and the treatment of the young offender (between the ages say of seventeen and twenty-three) has led to the increasing involvement of probation oficers in these fields – indeed they are now officially known as 'probation and after-care officers'.

Contacts between probation officers and schools will thus continue to take place when the children involved are in the top classes of the secondary schools; but it seems likely that because of the demands made by adult offenders, POs will less and less be able to offer an advisory service to juveniles and their teachers.

It should also be remembered, however, that the service is still the largest marriage guidance agency in the country (because of the officers' involvement in matrimonial disputes which come before the courts); and that a number of POs have been seconded to the divorce courts to advise on such vexed questions as custody of the children of the marriage.

Health services

Teachers will be well aware of the services offered by the school's medical officer and nurse and of the ways in which to use them appropriately. Where these people are long-serving, an affectionate relationship springs up and they can offer understanding and wise counsel on non-medical problems. The recent reorganization of the National Health Service should not affect these relationships, though some doctors may reappear under new titles.

An important figure in the reorganized service is that of the specialist in community medicine (child health). He – or quite often she – will be responsible for the development of a comprehensive service for pre-school and school-age children in an area; and a Health Area corresponds broadly with a County Council, or Education Authority, area.

Another important figure is the district community physician. A Health District – quite different from the local government District – is fairly large and based on the notional catchment area of a hospital, that is, a population of about 200,000. The DCP, along with a district nursing officer, administrator and finance officer, is responsible for the management of *all* the services in the District, whether hospital-based or community-based, whether for schoolchildren or for senior citizens. Among his manifold duties are the establishment of health care planning teams (to survey existing provision and prepare development plans) and the servicing of the Community Health Councils which provide lay 'oversight' of the organization. Teachers may find themselves involved in either or both of these activities.

Medical staff attached to schools may of course offer invaluable support and advice in many situations and are also in a position to mobilize other medical services – e.g., psychiatric and paediatric specialists. They also have an important role to play in 'screening' children through routine medical checks. Disturbed or disruptive behaviour is sometimes linked with physical conditions such as abnormal brain-rhythms or defective hearing, and it is to be hoped that children with actual or incipient impairments can be 'spotted' early and kept under surveillance.

Youth and community service

It is difficult to describe this service because it is organized in many different ways and its officers often interpret their brief in different ways.

The service has its roots in the Youth Club movement, and the maintenance of a network of activities, both formal and unorthodox, for teenagers is still a mainstream activity. The Albemarle Report of 1960, however, widened the movement's scope altogether by envisaging its involvement, in the whole continuum of human growth and development and with the needs and interactions of different age-groups. Thus within one County one may find one youth and community officer concentrating on the drug-problem in terms of 'secondary prevention' and another involved in services for elderly people in order to arouse the interest of youngsters in their needs.

In many places fresh approaches and experimental ventures are being initiated in order to 'reach out' to youngsters who spurn orthodox modes of conduct. Many of them are of school age. Some 'detached' youth workers – for instance, those who have no club building as a base but who contact youngsters in pubs or on street corners – may often be involved in a counselling relationship with an individual schoolchild. However the confidential nature of that relationship may preclude any 'feedback' to the child's teacher.

To the handling of disturbed children within the school setting the youth worker may have no contribution to make. He is, however, in possession of unrivalled information about the opportunities which exist in a locality to engage the interest of a wayward youngster and divert his energies into socially acceptable channels. Moreover, he may be able to advise on extra-curricular activities within the school to supplement those resources.

Voluntary societies

No account of the supportive services, even as brief a one as this, could omit mention of the voluntary bodies, though they are so various and complex that it is impossible to give a comprehensive account. None, perhaps, provides a direct service to help in dealing with disruptive youngsters. However, the work of the NSPCC in protecting children subject to physical abuse is well-known; not quite so well known is the work of its inspectors in 'preventive' social work designed to help families who are at risk. The Samaritans – in which no doubt many teachers play a part – report an increasing number of calls for help from children of school age. Many organizations raise funds and provide facilities for special groups of children, particularly those suffering from different types of handicap. There are also mutually-supportive groups, for instance those of parents of mentally handicapped children. Children from one-parent families are to be found in schools in increasing numbers, and single parents can be greatly helped by such organizations as Gingerbread. There are also a number of grant-making bodies, charitable trusts and so on, from which help can be obtained for families whose problems are financial. On the whole it can be said that there has been a distinct shift recently within the voluntary movement into the field of secondary prevention, but the result of this will not be seen for some considerable time.

Social Security

Up to now we have discussed those services which might be described as 'personal' in that they rely on the influence of one person in a relationship with another. Such services can differ markedly from one place to another since they rely on alternative priorities, personal judgments and so on. Social Security is 'impersonal', in that the system relies on the application of rules and criteria and is uniform across the country. It does not of course provide support and counsel to the teacher dealing with a problem child, but it does provide support to the stricken family – for example to the widow or deserted mother with young children to bring up.

As was said at the beginning of this chapter, the reasons why children become disturbed and disruptive are many and varied; but there seems to be a correlation, though by no means a cast-iron one, between personality problems and poverty. Many problem children come from families existing for one reason or another on Social Security; and although nobody pretends that Social Security benefits permit much more than subsistence living, the system is so complicated that few claimants realize the full extent of the benefits to which they are *entitled*. Allowances for the maintenance of children's clothing at a reasonable level are for example not always claimed; nor is the system of Family Income Supplements widely understood.

It may be rare for teachers to find themselves in a position in which they can offer advice to parents about what might generally be called 'income maintenance'. Where however there seems to be hardship which is affecting children advice and guidance could be tactfully offered. As a general guide to the income maintenance system it is recommended that schools equip themselves with a free booklet, *Family Benefits and Pensions*, obtainable from the DHSS (Leaflets Unit), Block 2, Government Buildings, Honeypot Lane, Stanmore, Middlesex HA7 1AY.

These then are the instruments of the supportive services. No one will pretend that there are not gaps, duplications, lapses in communication and a persistent shortage of resources. Nevertheless, let us examine what happens when the instruments begin playing together. Let us take the story of an entirely fictitious family, the Smiths of Smith Street.

Tommy Smith enters his primary school at the age of ten: he is a surly, bullet-headed little boy and the head teacher's heart sinks as he regards him and the thin, jumpy, bottle-blonde mother who accompanies him. Preliminary enquiries establish that the family has just moved into Smith Street from a distant part of the country, and preliminary testing shows that Tommy is already two to three years retarded in his attainments.

When the school records are eventually assembled, it is revealed that the family have had numerous addresses during the past five years and that Tommy is truly only 'known as Smith' and that his real name is something else. By this time concern is already filtering up to the head about Tommy's behaviour outside the classroom and there have been complaints about younger children being terrorized into handing over sweets.

The school staff makes arrangements to contain the situation, including the fostering of Tommy's only apparent talent, that of playing football; and the first move to invoke the supportive services is related to Tommy's younger half-brother Kenny. Kenny's attendance at school is becoming increasingly erratic, and the head's invitation to the mother to come and discuss the situation is ignored. The education welfare officer is asked to call.

The EWO's report reveals that there are two more children, below school age, and that the family occupy a grotty two-room flat at the top of a grotty terraced house. The mother is harassed and depressed and admits that she is again pregnant; the husband is not in evidence. Mrs Smith says she always gets Kenny off to school in good time but the demands of the youngest children prevent her from seeing that he actually gets there. She wearily assures the EWO that she will try harder.

Halfway through the summer term Kenny's attendance falls away completely; and during the summer holidays Tommy gets into trouble. He is 'found on enclosed premises', in fact in a yard at the back of a corner shop, one August evening: the police administer an official caution.

In the autumn Tommy proceeds into secondary school, accompanied by a gloomy report from his late head; and before many months are out the school staff are expressing concern about his association with the most turbulent and least well endowed of his peers. In fact a gang is forming, first in the playground, then outside the school gates, then actually within the classroom: an insolent bravado seems to link its members. It comes as no surprise to anyone when a note arrives from the Social Services Department asking for a school report to be incorporated in the social enquiry report: Tommy is to be brought before the juvenile court.

The social worker's report goes to the magistrates, not to the head. It reveals a good deal more about the family. The parents are not married to each other: both are refugees from previous cohabitations and indeed this one seems to be breaking down as the man is more often out of the flat than in it. Money is scarce, the new baby is grizzling and pasty-faced, there are rent arrears but there is a new colour telly. Although the situation is parlous, the social worker nevertheless points out that Tommy has had such numerous changes of school and home that his best chance of survival seems to lie in some continuity of care and treatment, together with an effort to tackle the family's multifarious problems. There is no mention of Kenny.

The magistrates make a supervision order, but the head teacher is not informed. The social worker makes a first shot at tackling the family problems, but comes up immediately against that of accommodation. Mrs Smith can scarcely cope where she is, but as a new arrival in a district with thousands of families on the housing waiting list there is no hope of a solution within 'the public sector'. The best the social worker can do for the time being is to get the two pre-school children into a local playgroup, to give their mother some relief and to give them a kind of therapeutic experience. The whole situation is complicated by Mr Smith: because he is now only loosely connected with the family, Mrs Smith can get neither adequate money out of him nor a dependable income from Social Security.

At this stage, unbeknown to each other, the EWO is trying to cope with Kenny's persistent non-attendance, the social worker with Tommy's behaviour and use of leisure time, and the health visitor with the care of the baby, Dawn, who is now a miserable underweight little thing in as near a neurotic condition as a baby can get. To add to the confusion the social worker, a kindly young man with a genuine liking for boys such as Tommy, is obliged by domestic pressures to go for promotion elsewhere; and the only replacement available is a practical down-to-earth middle-aged woman whom Tommy distrusts on sight. The boy's behaviour in school becomes more and more negative: he has not yet reached the violent or disruptive stage but he is drifting beyond the reach of anything the school can offer, and even the attempts of a young male teacher to befriend him fail because Tommy has by now had so many 'uncles' that he cannot trust any of them. Anyway, it is a large school and the head is too much bothered by the immediate problems of his fifteen-year-olds to be able to switch any resources to the first year.

In real life, such messy uncoordinated situations can drift on for years and it would be dishonest to pretend otherwise. Nor can certain intractable problems be wished away: the shortage of housing, the miserable semi-cohabitation. Nevertheless let us jump to the point at which some coordinated effort becomes possible.

This comes when Tommy gets into serious trouble and does literally hundreds of pounds' worth of damage to his own school: breaking and entering it in search of money leads to vandalism and then to arson. The magistrates remand him to the care of the Social Services Department with a request for full reports, and he is sent to an assessment centre. It is here that the situation is really taken apart and information is sought from all quarters. Tommy's head is asked to supply not a brief report for the court but a full-scale educational appraisal for a professional colleague; medical, psychological, psychiatric and social reports are obtained; case conferences are called to which Tommy's teachers are invited. It is discovered at this late stage that Mr Smith is on probation and the probation officer's views are sought. Enquiries are made as to whether Tommy's 'real' father can be traced, though this effort proves abortive; but through this enquiry his grandparents are located and they make positive gestures of interest and concern.

The problem of Tommy is seen as the immediate one. His needs are for remedial education, for self-esteem and success, for close relationships with father-figures and with mother-figures and for control. A care order is recommended with a view to placing him at one of the smaller community schools. The help of the grandparents is invoked and they are offered help with the cost of travelling so that they can visit Tommy regularly.

In order to secure his family base for him, social work support to the mother is vital; and although Kenny is not the immediate concern of the assessment centre team, it has now become clear that the social worker must be seen as 'the conductor of the orchestra of services'. The help of the school psychological service is obtained to transfer Kenny to a special day school with transport laid on to get him there.

Fortuitously, Tommy's 'trouble' upsets Mr Smith so much that he departs, the probation officer agreeing not to try to get him back. Mrs Smith is literally taken by the hand to the Social Security offices and her income put on a reliable though not lavish basis: immediate discretionary grants help her to get the younger children clothes and bedding.

Firm medical and social reports are sent to the housing manager who, harassed though he is by scores of 'top priority' cases, nevertheless agrees to seek halfway or substandard accommodation for Mrs Smith so that at least she will have more room while awaiting a better and more permanent solution.

The EWO is allotted the task of watching over the two little girls who come next in the family with a view to securing their early admission to school and the provision of free meals; the school medical service will in due course pay particular attention to the needs of these two.

There is a great debate about the baby, Dawn. The social worker maintains that the child has a right to remain in her family circle and the mother's level of care should be improved; the health visitor maintains that the baby was unwanted and the mother has little maternal feeling, so 'before it is too late' the baby should be placed for adoption. It is known that the mother is wavering in her feelings and would agree, rather dully, to either course of action.

It may be best to leave this intriguing problem before the reader, inviting him to make his own mind up about a situation which in one form or another confronts social workers every day. Dawn is not of immediate concern to teachers: but in due course she will come into the school system, and teachers will reap the harvest of whatever seeds are sown now.

Of more immediate concern in the case of Tommy. It will be seen from his story that things really had to get into a serious state before people sat down and began talking effectively about him. Maybe they should have started talking before ever he arrived in Smith Street; but when, and to what purpose? He was conceived before his parents made an ill-fated marriage; he was lagging on his developmental milestones before he was through his infant school, but what harassed social worker, struggling with numerous disturbed adolescents, could have intervened before the parents themselves even perceived that they had a problem?

In short, given that no service is going to get any more resources, how do we maximise the resources that we have got?

References

JORDAN, W. (1972) *The Social Worker in Family Situations* London: Routledge and Kegan Paul

KELLMER PRINGLE, M. L. (1971) *Deprivation and Education* London: Longman

SMITH N. J. (1972) *A Brief Guide to Social Legislation* London: Methuen

STROUD, J. (1975) *Where to Get Help* London: Ward Lock Educational

STROUD, J. (ed.) (1973) *Services for Children and Their Families* Oxford: Pergamon

WILLMOTT, P. (1973) *Consumers Guide to British Social Services* Harmondsworth: Penguin

Note

[1] The Children Act of 1975, though not at the time of writing fully implemented, does however extend and strengthen the power of control.

11 Education in personal relationships

D. R. POOLE
Adviser in Personal Relationships, Gloucestershire

Disruption is a crisis point. Is it realistic to consider only crisis? Disruption is a popular word to describe a variety of manifestations of indiscipline, having a wide range of interpretation. Is it sufficiently positive to consider what we do only at a time of crisis? Is it not much more effective to consider what is responsible for the crisis?

There is currently much concern about the difficulties presented by disruption in schools, to which possibly a disproportionate amount of time is being given. Greater significance should be devoted to thoughtful ways of preventing their development. Disruption is often a result of a fundamental breakdown in relationships. It would be wiser to devote attention to a greater understanding of relationships by the pupils and by the teachers who, whether or not they are directly involved in a programme of education in personal relationships, must be aware of the significance of their own attitudes and the way in which they relate to colleagues and pupils. Disruption relates to a growing number of pupils, but it should be remembered that a proper understanding of relationships is a concern of all pupils and not only of the minority which presents extreme difficulties.

The ideas outlined should be regarded as fundamental to all pupils, regardless of ability, and it is in this wider context that consideration will be given to the causes of disruption, to the ways in which matters of relationships might be discussed by pupils, and to accepting that there will be a minority for whom crisis might well be inevitable.

From the many cases of disruptive behaviour studied, it is apparent that a major cause of difficulty is a breakdown in relationships between the child and the adults with whom he comes into contact. Let us take an example of a parent's inability to understand the development into adulthood of a young person. John, an intelligent, sensitive boy of fifteen with well reasoned, if not always socially acceptable, views was extremely disruptive and was suspended from school. He was received voluntarily into care and, after a period in a community school, transferred into a second secondary school where after a short period of settled behaviour he was again extremely disruptive, resulting in a further suspension. John had every reason to believe that he should be disruptive. He himself expressed the view with considerable conviction that he had been given this role and was determined to act it out. A closer examination of the reasons behind his difficulties showed, quite clearly, that there was a lack of understanding on the part of his parents, particularly his father, about his growing up. John's father was angry at his son's apparent inability to meet expectations and ideals considered by him to be of worth. He lacked sensitivity and real understanding for John and a violent situation arose. Schools bore the brunt of John's frustration.

A member of staff may find himself at the point of crisis through no fault of his own. A pupil with a long record of difficult behaviour may provoke an unfortunate response from an unprepared teacher, and this is demonstrated by an incident in which a teacher was irritated by a boy's lack of cooperation and lethargy on entering a room. The boy was pushed, retaliated by being particularly abusive, which ultimately required his suspension from school. Teachers and pupils alike should be aware of moments of potential explosion.

The personal stress experienced by Richard in what he considered to be a very real relationship with his girlfriend within the school demonstrates another form of dilemma, exhibiting itself in disruption. Members of staff were aware of, and to a sensible degree were in sympathy with, Richard's attachment, which was seen to offer a degree of stability that the boy required. Such was the strength of this relationship that Richard became over-sensitive and over-protective to the girl, causing the staff to react perhaps unwisely. Richard, in his need to maintain the relationship, precipitated his suspension by becoming violent and abusive to his peers and members of staff.

It may well be impossible to prevent all cases of disruption, but the examples given, and there could be many more, demonstrate that efforts ought to be made to consider the implications, the pressures and the difficulties of adolescent development. There must be an opportunity for the pupil to consider himself and his relationship with others. It is insufficient to regard this process as one with which pupils will automatically and successfully come to terms. Opportunities need to be created in which the pupil is able to consider development of personal freedom, whilst appreciating that this implies a strong sense of responsibility. Adult and sexual roles require considerable explanation, discussion and questioning if there is to be a chance that they will be understood.

Perhaps the most difficult area of adolescent development is an appreciation of self-awareness and self-knowledge. Equally, it is exceedingly difficult for adolescent pupils to accept imperfections and limitations. Is it reasonable to expect them to possess insight without having had the opportunity to test their abilities? Decision-making is not an easy exercise, and young people must be very confused by what appear to be complexities introduced by adults in what, for the young person, must seem to be a very straightforward and logical step. In situations of stress, self-control will be very difficult. In his bid for independence, the adolescent needs to come to terms with these factors in order to become an adult with an identifiable role. Undoubtedly, help needs to be given, not only to those who may be experiencing particular difficulties but to every pupil who will be going through this inescapable period. In the development of role identity, the process already described will manifest itself by the individual exhibiting behavioural patterns, some of which will be irksome and some of which will be acceptable in society. Here the factors which lead to the crisis of disruption, for example, lack of interest, rebellion, violence, vandalism, are of particular concern. More positively, in attempts to enable the pupil to establish acceptable relationships, it will be necessary to consider, in the attainment of role identity, factors such as the willingness to accept commitment, quest for personal ethic, social responsibility, personal dedication to a cause, team activity and service to others.

To provide an adequate programme of education in personal relationships, the base of which has been described, teachers will require in-service education in which provision is made for learning the appropriate skills, receiving additional factual information and for opportunities to discuss with colleagues the implications of education in personal relationships. An in-service programme for teachers must include an examination of counselling methods, group discussion techniques and guidance on the difficult task of answering appropriately pupils' questions.

Since the basis of education in personal relationships is adolescent psychological development, it is in this area that teachers will require particular help. Similarly, sexuality, deviations, violence, vandalism, excessive use of alcohol, contraception, abortion and illegitimacy are topics in which teachers will need additional information and guidance about how this information can effectively and with sensitivity be imparted to pupils. It would be wrong to assume that the entire responsibility for such work with young people rests exclusively with teachers. They too must be aware of limitations and appreciate that other agencies and departments, for example, Area Health Authority, Social Services Department, police, the probation and after-care service, have a great deal of expertise and can successfully play a part in programmes of personal relationships in schools. More will be said later about the involvement of parents. It will be a function of the in-service courses to identify for teachers the work of such agencies. The administration of schools varies to such a degree that to suggest a rigid programme of personal relationships is impracticable. Guidance on various approaches which allow for modification to suit particular needs must be given. The issues that are likely to be raised will not only receive attention in personal relationships sessions; other areas of the curriculum will, quite naturally, overlap and every effort must be made to avoid unnecessary duplication or complete omission. The in-service programme is only able to produce a beginning: there will be limitations of time and teachers must recognize the need for further periods of in-service education, together with reading and the collection of resource material to support them in their work.

Though all teachers should be aware of this significant aspect of their role, the depth of involvement suggested will not appeal to all; likewise there will be teachers whose talents would be best used in other directions. Teachers responsible for education in personal relationships must possess qualities of commitment, responsibility, integrity, compassion and humility and have the support of their school. The teacher responsible for personal relationships programmes should be working to achieve the following aims:

1   To inform the adolescent about himself and his growing powers of mind and body.
2   To help him to form and develop stable relationships with others and to be able to accept other people as they are.
3   To help him to face common situations and relationships with authority, parents, employers, workmates and with the other sex.
4   To remind him of the problems of humanity and to awaken an awareness of his responsibility towards his neighbours.
5   To help him to lay the foundations for marriage and family life.
6   To act as counsellor and guide to those in need, recognizing those who require specialist treatment.
7   To create a belief in schools that these things are important and are regarded as such by head and staff.

In the school situation the head must have full confidence in what the teacher is doing and give him ungrudging support. There must also be time for teachers of personal relationships to explain aspects of their work and to enlist the support of other members of staff. Although in some schools the personal relationships teacher may not carry his colleagues on the staff with him all the way, it is hoped that he will maintain their respect by the sincerity of his approach to his work. Furthermore, shoddiness in any of his work will seriously affect his influence in personal relationships.

Parents must have sufficient confidence in the teacher to permit him to reinforce what is essentially a family function. Teaching in the school must be an extension of family learning.

The teacher should regard himself quite humbly as a servant of the pupil's needs. His authority will emerge from such a relationship rather than by the adoption of an authoritarian attitude.

As well as the provision of in-service education and assistance offered by other agencies the teacher must have an opportunity to decide, after some initial involvement, whether he really feels that such work is his line of country. In considering a programme of in-service education, therefore, attention must be drawn in the early stages of the programme to what is required. Teachers will be given the opportunity to express their reasons for involvement in personal interviews. There will be the chance to discuss, in the small group situation, controversial issues. Those staffing the conference will be anxious to press the teachers to consider where they really stand on many personal and controversial issues. This approach is necessary because, in the school, pupils will not be hesitant in raising such issues. At this stage therefore the teacher must be able to withdraw if he so desires or indeed if, after discussion with the staff of the conference, it is considered best that he should not become involved in such depth in this work in schools. Within the programme there must be sessions covering the following areas, both in the form of lectures and discussions in small groups: the psychology of adolescence and the techniques of group discussion exercises; counselling the individual, for the teacher of personal relationships will undoubtedly be required to counsel on a one to one basis; sexuality and deviations, police attitudes, violence and vandalism, the juvenile liaison bureau, social service links, the probation and after-care service, extreme examples manifested by disruptive pupils, the place of personal relationships in the school setting and the importance of the ethos of the school.

In the classroom the personal relationships teacher must adopt a series of techniques if he is to be successful. He will have to obtain rapport with his group, so he must not be faced with impossible and difficult conditions. For example, his group should not be too large, the room should provide an informal and relaxed atmosphere, and if at all possible his discussion periods should not be at the mercy of timetable expediency and should remain uninterrupted.

The personal relationships teacher will have to spend a proportion of his time on factual teaching, so he must have a clear knowledge of his facts and the ability to impart them effectively. He needs to be able to accept questions, to give clear and helpful answers, and he must be a good listener. Dealing with children's questions is part of the everyday business of a teacher, and requires as much in the way of preparation as does the formal imparting of knowledge. Indeed, the child's question is its response to the teaching situation and may require further information or explanation of information already given or, at a deeper level, the definition of the teacher's attitude towards a problem or situation. Again, the child may be testing out the teacher, probing the teacher's depth of knowledge or sincerity of attitude. However the question-answer situation is viewed it is an opportunity for the establishment of a relationship between pupil and teacher.

Questions are about life and living and hence have emotional overtones. These things matter to the questioner and his questions are mostly not to satisfy idle curiosity. Again, some of the questions may be delicate and private, and shy children may be precluded from asking directly in front of their class; there must be an opportunity for such questions to be asked anonymously. Pupils must be able to trust the personal relationships teacher completely, and the answers to their questions will do much to encourage them. The task of the teacher is to persuade the young to realize their responsibilities and to keep a sense of normality. The aim is always to help them to form attitudes towards life, and the answers to questions should be wider than detailed statements of facts. So we consider what lies behind the question and listen carefully, taking all questions seriously, and avoiding flippant and 'off the cuff' answers. The teacher's attitude will set the tone of the sessions, and he or she should not be shocked by questions or condemn or condone people's weaknesses. On the other hand high drama must be avoided – strive for good humour and an understanding. Questions will essentially fall into three groups: fact-seeking; attitudes; and values. It is possible to anticipate some questions and the teacher must be well prepared and able to refute gross generalizations.

Much of the time will be spent in informal discussion with the group, and the importance of the techniques involved in group discussion work cannot be too highly emphasized. The teacher must have sympathy with the group and he must know its background; he must be prepared for questions of an unexpected nature and in meeting them to show himself to be unshockable and to have a quick sense of humour. He must be conversant with the attitudes of the young and understand the language they use. He must recognize the rich and infinite variety of human beings. In working with the young he must not enter into judgment or condemnation but rather encourage in them the capacity to make moral choices. He must give himself a source of reference to which he must return periodically to reorientate his own thinking. He must keep himself up to date by reading and reflecting on his own attitudes and beliefs in the light of changing circumstances.

Possibly the hardest thing a teacher is called upon to do in group work is to express his own conviction, firmly and sincerely. Young people recognize and appreciate sincere convictions and are quick to see through superficial hearsay just as they resent too authoritarian a presentation of the teacher's beliefs.

Personal relationships are an area in which there should be meaningful exchange with parents. Many teachers say that schools are increasingly being asked to undertake parental responsibilities. Parents' meetings provide opportunities to discuss the programme of personal relationships within the school and provide a wide forum for discussion of issues such as discipline, in which quite clearly the school is unable to accept the responsibility to society as a whole.

This provides scope for parallel developments in the community. Discussion work might well be introduced into many adult groups – a school PTA is an obvious example. Trained voluntary workers operating in this way could provide valuable support to a school scheme of personal relationships and create in the community an awareness of the importance of such work in schools.

With an established schools scheme there should be an in-service education programme for youth service personnel. They too, like the parents, will need to be aware of the work of schools and be in a position to offer help directly to young people on both an individual and group basis.

There must be coordination of effort and an understanding of the approaches used by the many agencies concerned with the successful personal development of young people. Local liaison groups representing education, health, police, probation, social services and youth provide a valuable forum for discussing difficulties caused by disruption and other allied problems.

Although schools may have a programme of personal relationships as outlined it would be naive not to recognize the fact that there will be on occasions serious breakdowns of relationships, with pupils expressing extreme degrees of disruptive behaviour. Other methods may therefore have to be adopted, other agencies quickly called in able to deal with specialist problems; nor may the normal day school be considered suitable for some pupils. If extreme disruption occurs then schools will look for additional support. An Authority may require a scheme to provide this support. Schools should retain normal rights and responsibilities for discipline including short periods of suspension. In any scheme flexibility must be retained so that it can be modified to suit particular circumstances.

The following is therefore suggested as a model for application after the usual sanctions, which may have already included suspension and/or interview with parents. Parents and pupil should be interviewed at school, perhaps with governors or a sub-committee of governors, and the parents will be warned about suspension or further suspension and about the reference of the issue to the Education Authority. If such a school-based interview is not adequate then there should be opportunity for parents and pupil to be interviewed again, this time at the Education Office before a panel representative of both office and school personnel and, of course, any other agencies already involved with the pupil or family. At this stage, the seriousness of the matter should be emphasized by suggesting transfer to a second school and subsequently some form of court action. A further breakdown may well require a second interview at the Education Department at which arrangements will be made for transfer to a second school. The second school will be of considerable importance in as much as it will have to attempt to give the transferred pupil, despite his very difficult record, a genuinely fresh start. It is at this stage that final warnings are given, but if a further breakdown occurs then the Education Authority or another agency will seek the sanction of the courts. The effectiveness of court action as an ultimate deterrent leaves something to be desired, both because the difficulties in prosecuting parents and because of the limited effect of the options available to a juvenile court. A court must not be seen as the solution of all problems.

A disruptive pupil who has been before the courts and possibly spent time in a community school will quite probably be recommended for return to school, as with young people who have been away from day school as a result of court action or being received into care. Such pupils will require much attention and the resources of schools will be strained to provide proper and caring help.

Discussions about the desirability of returning such pupils and its timing, together with effective placement, will require the full involvement of an Education Authority with the Social Services Department and the staff of the institution which the young person is leaving. It is insufficient for contact to be made with the Education Authority only when the young person is back in his own locality and educational provision is required.

The scheme of personal relationships already described, together with its links at youth and community levels, has been in operation in Gloucestershire for thirteen years. During this time many teachers have become involved and considerable experience gained. It is a field in which review is regularly necessary, for if the scheme is to be meaningful it must reflect the needs and interests of the times; it must be aware of social trends and responsive to change.

The problem of disruption is with us and a scheme of personal relationships must respond to this latest challenge. It would be wrong to suggest however that it is, or even that it can be, a complete answer. It gives an opportunity, if incorporated fully into the work of the school, for the pupils to be helped in their attempt to come to terms with themselves and their relationships with others. These, regardless of academic attainment, will be an inescapable feature of their life.